NATIVE PLANTS
for New England Gardens

NATIVE PLANTS
for New England Gardens

Dan Jaffe and Mark Richardson
Photographs by Dan Jaffe

NEW ENGLAND
WILD
FLOWER
SOCIETY

Globe
Pequot
Guilford, Connecticut

Globe Pequot

An imprint of Rowman & Littlefield

Distributed by NATIONAL BOOK NETWORK

Copyright © 2018 Rowman & Littlefield
Photos by Dan Jaffe unless otherwise noted

British Library Cataloguing in Publication Information available

Library of Congress Cataloging-in-Publication Data
Names: Richardson, Mark, 1978- author.
Title: Native plants for New England gardens / Mark Richardson ; photographs by Dan Jaffe.
Description: Guilford, Connecticut : Globe Pequot, [2018] | Includes index. |
    Identifiers: LCCN 2017035997 (print) | LCCN 2017048678 (ebook) | ISBN
    9781493029266 (e-book) | ISBN 9781493029259 (pbk.)
Subjects: LCSH: Native plants for cultivation—New England. | Endemic
    plants—New England.
Classification: LCC SB439 (ebook) | LCC SB439 .R53 2018 (print) | DDC
    635.9/5174—dc23
LC record available at https://lccn.loc.gov/2017035997

Printed in the United States of America

CONTENTS

INTRODUCTION

Few things reflect the unique character of New England like its native plants. Native plants not only provide beauty and highlight the distinctiveness of a region, but they also help to support healthy ecosystems, providing habitat for local wildlife. Native plants evolved over millennia within a region's environment, making them well adapted to a particular place, and so when properly sited in a garden, they require fewer inputs like irrigation, fertilizer, and pesticides to remain healthy. As our landscapes become more developed and the space between wild areas grows wider and wider, it is critical that we think of our managed landscapes, like the gardens we all care for, as more than just ornamentation. Our gardens are critical ecosystems, providing habitat for wildlife, capturing and filtering stormwater, and sequestering carbon. Native plants are fundamental components of these urban and suburban ecosystems, and by using more of them in our gardens, we can keep our environment healthy and celebrate the charm of the region we call home, New England.

DEFINING NATIVE

For those of us who work with native plants professionally, defining what we mean by "native" can be a colossal challenge unto itself. Generally speaking, native is defined by "where" and "when." In other words, native plants are considered to be those that existed in a given location at a specific point in time. The first point, location, is simple enough, but requires that you choose parameters. From broad terms like "North American native" to narrow terms like "native to Middlesex County, Massachusetts," the gardener, landscape designer, or horticulturist sets the criteria and chooses plants that fit. At Garden in the Woods, New England Wild Flower Society's native plant botanic garden in Framingham, Massachusetts, and for the purposes of selecting plants for this book, native plants are those that naturally occur in the US Environmental Protection Agency's (EPA) Ecoregions of New England (see map, Appendix B). According to the EPA, "Ecoregions are areas where ecosystems (and the type, quality, and quantity of environmental resources) are generally similar." The original framework for ecoregions was developed by James Omernik in the 1980s. Ecoregions describe large regions that share similar climates, geology, hydrology, and so on. This method for selecting native plants based not on political boundaries (state and county lines, for example), but on ecological boundaries, more closely resembles plant distribution and allows the gardener to choose plants that share similar cultural requirements, having adapted together over millennia.

The second point, when, is a little more complicated and can be a bit more controversial. For simplicity's sake, we define native as dating back to European settlement. In other words, if a plant was in an area at the time the first European settlers arrived, it is considered native. While using a rigid time parameter implies that natural plant migration halted when the pilgrims arrived, it also makes it easy to determine which plants migrated on their own and which were introduced from outside the region. Species migrate constantly; in fact, every plant in our flora migrated northward since the last ice age, a mere ten thousand to twelve thousand years ago. When plants migrate into an area on their own, they do so slowly, typically by natural movement of seed by wind, animals, and water. Natural migration is obstructed by geographic barriers, like oceans and mountain ranges. When people move plants, they can do so across great distances, moving plants across oceans, mountain ranges, and the like. While the vast majority of introduced plants are innocuous and don't ever escape cultivation, there are myriad examples of introduced plants that have escaped cultivation and become invasive.

Invasive species are those that are non-native and whose growth disrupts or causes harm to minimally managed ecosystems. Invasive species are not simply garden thugs that take over a perennial border, like lily-of-the-valley (*Convallaria majalis*); rather, invasive species are those that cause substantial harm to natural lands, like oriental bittersweet (*Celastrus orbiculatus*). Invasive plants are sometimes garden runaways, like burning bush (*Euonymus alatus*), while others were imported for soil stabilization, like kudzu (*Pueraria montana*). Working with native plants is one great way to ensure the plants in your garden will not contribute to the disastrous environmental and economic effects of invasive species, which are estimated to cost the United States over $120 billion annually.

RIGHT PLANT FOR THE RIGHT PLACE

It's easy to get lost in a garden center, admiring the various colors and textures and thinking about where that great new plant with its steel-blue flowers might look best in your garden. Gorgeous plants can be hard to resist. The temptation to buy that attractive new plant without first thinking about whether it's compatible with your garden is difficult to avoid. We've all been there. Wandering through the garden center, your eye is immediately drawn to that shrub with bright red flowers. On the way to the cash register to check out, that tall tree with star-shaped leaves calls out to you. Before you know it, that groundcover with the delicate foliage somehow finds its way into your shopping cart. You get everything home only to realize that all the plants you've just bought want full sun when all you have to offer is shade. Choosing native plants is one easy step toward knowing whether a plant will struggle or thrive in your garden, but it's not the only step. It's reasonable to assume a native plant will be hardy enough to survive our winters, and that it is not invasive. Beyond that, gardeners must think about that ever-important principle: the right plant for the right place.

All plants, regardless of their origin, have specific cultural requirements, and if planted in the wrong place will struggle to survive. The key is to visit the garden center armed with a good understanding of what your garden has to offer, and to choose plants based not only on their looks, but also on their cultural needs. Cardinal flower (*Lobelia cardinalis*) is stunning, but plant one in a dry, shady site and it will never flower. On the other hand, plant bearberry (*Arctostaphylos uva-ursi*) in a wet spot and it will rot. When selecting plants for gardens, the goal should be to put plants where they will require no supplemental irrigation once established (a period of two to three years, depending on the plant and the situation). To understand what your garden has to offer, consider three important factors: light, soil type/moisture, and space availability.

Consider full sun anything greater than six hours of direct sunlight per day. Anything less than six hours is some variation of part shade to shade. Conduct a simple light analysis by observing light and shadow at least three times throughout the day, for example, at 8 a.m., noon, and 4 p.m. Soil can be a little more difficult to evaluate. Determine how well your site drains by conducting a percolation test. The simplest method is to dig a hole about eight inches deep, fill it with water, let the water drain, and then fill it again. If it takes longer than twenty-four hours for the water to drain, your site is poorly drained; less than twelve hours, and your site is very well drained. Contact your local cooperative extension to conduct a soil analysis to determine your percent organic matter, soil texture, and pH. Finally, choose plants that at maturity will be the appropriate size for your garden. Avoid planting tall trees under power lines or planting aggressive spreading plants next to delicate, slow-growing specimens.

There is a steep learning curve for the beginning gardener, but building a thorough understanding of these three components of a garden is a huge step toward making the right decisions about which plants to choose. One final point: No matter what a plant's cultural requirements, all new plants require care to establish in the garden. Treat newly establishing plants as if they are still in a container, providing ample water at least for the first growing season to make sure they get off to a good start.

MAINTAINING THE ECOLOGICAL GARDEN

The ultimate goal for the ecological gardener is a beautiful garden that provides year-round interest, supports local wildlife, absorbs and filters rainwater, and improves air quality. In other words, the ecological gardener thinks not just about creating and maintaining a beautiful garden, but also about the garden's impact on environmental quality. At Garden in the Woods, we practice some basic principles that ensure our garden stewardship contributes positively to environmental quality.

First and most basic, we use native plants. As mentioned previously, native plants are fundamental components of healthy ecosystems. They provide habitat for wildlife as well as a beautiful display for people to admire.

Second, we limit our use of irrigation water to new plantings. We site plants properly, matching their cultural needs to the right places in the garden so that we can turn off the irrigation water once plants are established. As much as 30 percent of the potable water in New England is used for irrigating lawns and gardens. With droughts becoming more commonplace, it's critical that we decrease that percentage, and siting plants properly is the simplest step in that direction.

Next, we never use fertilizers in the garden, focusing instead on building healthy, organic soils that provide all the nutrition our plants require. Fertilizers, even when used responsibly, are pollutants; they are highly mobile forms of basic elements like nitrogen and phosphorus that cause direct environmental harm to waterways. Fertilizer runoff leads to algal blooms and ocean dead zones, and the reality is that by recycling organic waste through composting and using organic mulches in our gardens, we have no need of fertilizers.

Finally, we never use pesticides of any sort in the garden. Pesticides can have disastrous unintended consequences to human health, as well as catastrophic environmental impacts. Fourteen of the thirty most commonly used lawn pesticides are known neurotoxins or carcinogens, and two-thirds of them cause reproductive harm in humans. Those at particular risk are children and pets that come into direct contact with gardens and lawns treated with pesticides. Systemic pesticides, like those commonly referred to as "neonics," are absorbed by a plant's vascular system, making the entire plant toxic to harmful and beneficial insects alike. The use of systemic pesticides has been linked to the decline of important pollinators, and their widespread use in growing plants for gardens means that many important pollinator plants are toxic to the very insects gardeners intend to support. When buying plants, always ask whether or not they have been treated with systemic pesticides, and avoid using these products in your garden.

Ecological gardening with native plants is a fantastic way to keep our gardens beautiful and make sure they support healthy, local eco-systems. In the pages that follow, we hope you will keep all of these principles in mind as you consider adding some of these fabulous native plants to your garden.

Herbaceous Perennials

Herbaceous perennials are flowering plants, not including grasses and sedges, that live for more than one growing season but lack aboveground woody stems. Herbaceous perennials have belowground storage structures like rhizomes or corms that allow them to survive winter. Their aboveground stems and leaves normally die back to the ground each season. In New England, we have a rich diversity of herbaceous perennials, providing gardeners the ability to choose plants that flower from late March through October. Because they lack woody stems, herbaceous perennials can and should be planted closely together, with the intent of forming pseudo plant communities that knit together to cover bare soil and create a lower-maintenance garden. When designing perennial borders, combine plants that require similar growing conditions and bloom at various times of year for a long season of interest.

Baneberry and bugbane, *Actaea* spp.

The genus *Actaea* is a diverse group of perennials that can provide an attractive, long-lasting fruit display for a shady spot in the garden, or big, bold foliage and summer flowers. The genus is split into two main categories: the baneberries, which feature mildly showy flowers but persistent and attractive fruit, and the bugbanes, which feature very showy flowers in midsummer, but lack colorful fruit.

In New England, two species fall into the baneberry group. Red baneberry (*A. rubra*) blooms first and produces a deep, glossy red fruit that brightens the shade garden from midsummer through early fall. The berries are vibrant and contrast nicely with both the plant's dark foliage and the bright white fruit of its cousin, white baneberry, or doll's eyes (*A. pachypoda*). If red baneberry fruit is striking and beautiful, the fruit of doll's eyes borders on the surreal, almost creepy. Less pretty than fascinating, the pure white berries of doll's eyes are tipped with a dark black dot, giving the appearance of a cluster of eyes watching you wander through the garden.

Red baneberry and doll's eyes are very similar and difficult to distinguish from each other except when in fruit. Adding to the confusion of identification, each species has color forms, like the white form of red baneberry (*A. rubra* var. *neglecta*) or the red form of doll's eyes (*A. pachypoda* forma *rubrocarpa*). While this distinction might be important to botanists, the average gardener should simply enjoy the display and not worry too much about the details. Part sun to shade, average to moist soils, zones 3–8.

Formerly *Cimicifuga racemosa*, bugbane, or black cohosh (*A. racemosa*), is a tough plant for tough places. This summer-flowering species will grow happily under a dense canopy of white pine in dry, acidic soils, but is equally happy growing in rich, pH-neutral soils. Large white flower spikes shoot straight up in midsummer when few other native plants are in bloom. After flowering, black cohosh forms green fruits that are unremarkable at best and easily spread seed throughout the garden. To keep it from spreading throughout the garden, we recommend deadheading after flowering. Part shade to shade, average to moist soils, zones 4–9.

Black cohosh
PHOTO BY JACKIE DONNELLY

Wild onion, *Allium* spp.

When we think of onions, our minds are usually in the kitchen or in the vegetable garden. But there are some amazing native onions that most certainly belong in both the kitchen and the ornamental garden. Some native onions are showy enough to warrant planting for aesthetic value alone, while others are tasty enough to warrant festivals in their honor.

Nodding onion (*Allium cernuum*) is the most ornamental of the lot, but like most of its cousins, it is edible and delicious too. Used in cooking as a replacement for green onions or scallions, nodding onion can be harvested from the garden throughout the season. The entire plant is edible, but the leaves are far tastier than the bulb. They are tenderest when young, and continually cutting them for use in the kitchen will keep new, tender leaves growing all season. Plant some in the kitchen garden, but also grow it in the ornamental garden for a midsummer show of light to dark pink flowers that nod at the end of a tall flower stalk. Tolerant of sunny, dry sites, this plant will thrive in places where

Nodding onion

its cousins, wild garlic and ramps, don't survive. Sun to part shade, dry to average soils, zones 3–9.

Wild garlic (*A. canadense*) prefers moist soils, and although the flower is similar in texture to nodding onion, it is less colorful and stands erect, rather than nodding. Like nodding onion, the entire plant is edible, although in this case it's the bulbs that wild-food enthusiasts crave. The flavor is similar to mild kitchen garlic. Sun to part shade, average to moist soils, zones 3–9.

Though they make beautiful garden plants, it's the flavor of ramps, or wild leeks (*A. tricoccum*), that gets people talking. This is hands down one of the tastiest wild edibles in New England. Ramps taste like mild, sweet onions when eaten raw, making them a perfect addition to salad or for topping a piece of trout. They sweeten further when cooked, and have a texture reminiscent of lightly cooked spinach. They taste great served alone as a side dish (along with butter, garlic, and maybe some lemon zest), or wrapped around that trout, and they are fantastic in soups. With such a short season, they will never supplant culinary onion, but they are a phenomenal seasonal treat.

Ramps are rare in the wild, thanks at least in part to their popularity as a tasty edible, and should never be harvested from the wild. Thankfully, they are easy (albeit slow) to cultivate in a garden. Avoid eating the bulbs, which are far less tasty than the leaves anyway, and you'll be able to harvest them every spring. Part shade to shade, average to moist soils, zones 3–8.

Hepatica and windflower, *Anemone* spp.

The genus *Anemone* can be split into two distinct categories in New England—the hepaticas (which until recently were a separate genus altogether) and the windflowers. Sharp-lobed hepatica (*A. acutiloba*) and blunt-lobed hepatica (*A. americana*) are delicate woodland plants that are among the earliest natives to flower in spring. Their leaves emerge covered in dense hairs that are exquisitely textural as they unfurl. Leaves of both species are mottled, although the degree of mottling varies from one plant to the next. Flowers range from blue-violet to white, and, relative to the size of the plant overall, the flowers are quite large and very showy. Blunt-lobed hepatica is slightly more forgiving and easier to maintain in the garden than its cousin, sharp-lobed hepatica, which prefers richer soils. When properly sited, both species are long-lived and make a great choice for a shade garden. Part shade to shade, average to moist soils, zones 3–8.

Thimbleweed (*A. virginiana*) is happiest on dry slopes growing in gritty soils. Tolerant of blazing sun and very little water, thimbleweed fills a garden niche in which few other native plants can thrive. The flowers are attractive but are not nearly as showy as those of hepatica. The best ornamental attribute this plant has to offer is its thimble-shaped fruit, which forms soon after it has finished flowering, for the great texture it adds to the dry, sunny garden. As the fruits mature, they eventually dry and begin to fall apart, releasing thousands of small seeds attached to a light fluff that will carry them off in the air to find bare ground between cracks in rocks or other sandy places. Sun, dry to average soils, zones 2–9.

Canada windflower (*A. canadensis*) can be a great garden ally or a terrible garden thug depending on where it's planted. If you need a strongly spreading colonizer for a sunny moist spot, Canada windflower is a great choice. It's a perfect plant for covering a steep slope where it's foolish to keep trying to mow a lawn. Planted in drier or shadier spots, it can be a little tamer, but if you're looking for a delicate plant for a small spot in your garden, then look elsewhere. Densely lobed leaves give rise to stunning masses of pure white flowers in summer. A patch of Canada windflower can be breathtaking, but be sure to plant it somewhere that you won't mind it completely taking over. Sun to part shade, dry to moist soils, zones 2–9.

Thimbleweed fruit adds winter interest to a sunny spot in the garden.

Wild columbine, *Aquilegia canadensis*

There are plenty of reasons to plant wild columbine (*Aquilegia canadensis*), but perhaps none more compelling than its floral display. Wild columbine flowers are simply phenomenal. Vibrant red outer petals surround bright yellow inner petals that themselves surround a central mass of yellow stamens (male flower parts) and pistils (female flower parts). The petals are arranged into long tubes that produce healthy amounts of nectar deep inside the flower, out of reach of most bees and other insects. Because of this unique flower shape, the long narrow beak of a hummingbird or the long tongue of a butterfly is necessary to reach the tasty nectar reward.

Wild columbine blooms most heavily in spring, although some flowers will hold until early summer. After flowering, it produces dark black seeds that will find any small crack in a rock or a sliver of bare soil to germinate and grow into a new plant for next year's show. Because it's so easy to grow from seed, we recommend collecting it and spreading it around the garden, on path edges, in cracks between pavers, or anywhere your garden has a void that could use a little more spring color. Wild columbine is happy in average garden soils, but it also is extremely drought tolerant. Sun to part shade, dry to average soils, zones 3–9.

Red columbine

American spikenard has prolific fruit set in late summer.

American spikenard, *Aralia racemosa*

Here in New England, foundation plantings often get beaten down by the weight of winter snow sliding off a roof. At the end of a long, snowy winter, many shrubs and small trees planted too close to a house with a pitched roof have broken, dead, and dying branches. Rather than competing with nature and building elaborate snow covers to protect prized shrubs, it makes more sense to use herbaceous perennial plants in their place. American spikenard (*Aralia racemosa*) is one of those rare perennials that can resemble a shrub during the growing season because of its size (four to six feet tall and wide in the right conditions) and branching habit. But because it doesn't produce any woody stems, no amount of snow and ice can damage it over the winter.

In addition to its size and unique landscape character, American spikenard has giant compound leaves that contrast nicely with the plant's deep purple stems. Cream- to green-colored flowers appear in midsummer, and though hardly spectacular, they do lend a certain textural interest. The nondescript flowers are easily forgiven when the berries begin to form. Masses of small berries mature slowly, at first from green to red and then more quickly to a rich deep purple. The overall effect is almost like a fireworks display with green, red, and purple fruit simultaneously appearing before the whole mass turns purple.

The berries are edible and quite tasty, with both sweet and earthy flavors present. We love muddling them into cocktails (strain the seeds out after muddling or they'll float to the top of your drink) or just eating them right off the plant. Birds and chipmunks also are big fans, but the abundance of fruit makes it easy for you to get enough before they're gone.

Given its large, shrub-like form, its robust foliage, and its fabulous fruit display, we think every garden in New England should find space for at least one American spikenard. Part sun to part shade, average to moist soils, zones 3–8.

Jack-in-the-pulpit, *Arisaema triphyllum*

The great thing about Jack-in-the-pulpit (*Arisaema triphyllum*) is that it looks like it should be hard to grow. Having a healthy patch growing in a shady spot in the garden will make you the envy of many a gardening companion. On the contrary, however, it is an easygoing species that will handle just about any spot in the garden with a little shade and a little moisture. When growing in part sun and moist soil, Jack-in-the-pulpit can become quite robust, growing tall, with very large leaves. Beyond its striking appearance, Jack-in-the-pulpit is a downright cool plant once you get to know it a little better, thanks to an incredibly unique reproductive strategy.

Every Jack-in-the-pulpit seedling spends several years as a male plant, responsible only for pollen production, which is a relatively inexpensive investment when compared to fruit production. As seedlings continue to grow over several seasons, they store energy in the plant's belowground corm until they finally are large enough to support the relatively resource-intensive production of fruit. At this point, plants convert to female, producing a second leaf and female flowers, which give way to brilliant fruit. Jack-in-the-pulpit fruit is an upright, elongated bunch of vibrant red berries that last from late summer into fall and really pop in the shade of a woodland garden.

The flower, like the flowers of all plants in the arum family, including calla lily (*Calla palustris*) and skunk cabbage (*Symplocarpus foetidus*) is a spathe and spadix, which is why it's called Jack-in-the-pulpit. In this case, Jack (the spadix) is partially enclosed in the pulpit (the spathe). There are several color forms, ranging from almost pure green to white striped to deep red-purple. The perennial corms produce an annual root system, making it very easy to transplant once the plants have gone dormant in summer. Part shade to shade, average to moist soils, zones 3–9.

In New England, we find a closely related species called green dragon (*A. dracontium*) that is also worth planting. The leaves of green dragon are divided into nine to fifteen leaflets, and the green flowers contain a long "tongue" that attaches to the tip of the spadix and may aid in pollination. Green dragon is quite rare in the wild in New England and is far more site specific than Jack-in-the-pulpit. Part shade, moist soils, zones 3–9.

Jack-in-the-pulpit

Milkweed, *Asclepias* spp.

With all the recent attention paid to the plight of pollinators, milkweed (*Asclepias* spp.) has garnered increased interest as a great garden plant. In New England, the genus *Asclepias* consists of ten different native species, not all of which are worthy garden plants. Of those that are garden worthy, the three most commonly grown are common milkweed (*A. syriaca*), rose or swamp milkweed (*A. incarnata*), and butterfly milkweed (*A. tuberosa*).

If you happen upon an open field in New England and see thousands of milkweeds growing, then you are likely looking at common milkweed. Common milkweed is a colonizer, a strong spreading plant that is well suited to large open meadows, roadsides, hell strips, or as competition against invasive species. If you are looking for a well-behaved garden plant, then common milkweed is not the best choice. Like all milkweeds, it has striking little flowers, arranged in masses atop tall three- to four-foot stems. While it's not the best choice for the garden, common milkweed is the only milkweed we would recommend eating. Many of the plant's parts are edible and tasty, from young leaves to developing flower buds. Sun to part shade, dry to average soils, zones 3–9.

The milkweed that we most recommend for typical garden use is *A. incarnata*. Thanks to the descriptive but unfortunate common name, swamp milkweed, this plant is often thought of as needing to grow in wet soils. While in the wild it might only be found in wetlands, in the garden it is quite happy in average garden soil. We prefer the more pleasing moniker, rose milkweed, which more adequately describes it best attribute— beautiful, fragrant pink to purple flowers. Like all milkweeds found in New England, rose milkweed is the host plant for monarch butterfly caterpillars as well as tussock moths, swallowtails, and a variety of beneficial beetles. The plant seemingly supports whole ecosystems on its own, often playing host to bees, ants, and various spiders waiting to eat an unsuspecting pollinator. Sun to part sun, average to moist soils, zones 3–9.

If your garden's soils are on the dry side, then butterfly milkweed is probably your best choice. A tough plant for tough places, butterfly milkweed thrives in the driest of soils. Ornamentally, it is shorter than either common or rose milkweed, and has very attractive, deep green foliage in nice contrast to its brilliant orange-red flowers. Butterfly milkweed works great in combination with other dry-loving perennials like stiff aster (*Ionactis linariifolia*), little bluestem (*Schizachyrium scoparium*), and downy goldenrod (*Solidago puberula*). Sun to part sun, dry to average soils, zones 3–9.

The great spangled fritillary is one of many butterflies that feed on common milkweed.

Early blue cohosh

Blue cohosh, *Caulophyllum giganteum* and *Caulophyllum thalictroides*

There is good argument as to what time of year blue cohosh is at its showiest. Many folks contend that it is most attractive in early spring, as the garden awakens and new shoots emerge. At this time, blue cohosh unveils its small flowers as its leaves unfurl deep purple with a distinct yellow center in the case of early blue cohosh (*Caulophyllum giganteum*), green-yellow for blue cohosh (*C. thalictroides*). For early spring color, it's hard to find another plant that's equally attractive or unusual.

After its initial spring emergence, the leaves and stems of blue cohosh expand into a large open form with distinct gray-blue foliage. At this stage, it makes a superb textural element in the garden that works wonderfully in combination with later spring-blooming wildflowers like doll's eyes (*Actaea pachypoda*) or green and gold (*Chrysogonum virginianum*). In late spring, blue cohosh can be nondescript, paling against showier flowering plants like black cohosh, but it has another ornamental show in store in late summer and fall.

In late season, its green fruits mature to baby blue and resemble blueberries. Unfortunately, the fruits are not as tasty as they look—a large seed is encased just below the skin. Although they aren't edible, they put on quite a show in the garden, providing a splash of true blue, a color that is remarkably hard to find in the plant world.

Two different species of blue cohosh are found in New England. Both are fairly common in the horticultural trade, although confusion over identification abounds and both species are almost always labeled *C. thalictroides*. The deep purple color of early blue cohosh is certainly more attractive, but either of the two species makes a nice addition to a shady woodland garden. Part shade to shade, average to moist soils, zones 3–8.

White turtlehead, *Chelone glabra*

One of the most common misconceptions in gardening for pollinators is that attracting butterflies to a garden is all about flowers. While it is true that butterflies, like the Baltimore checkerspot, feed almost exclusively on nectar they gather from flowers, winged adults are merely the final stage in the butterfly life cycle. To attract butterflies to a garden, one must first provide habitat and host plants, those plant species that the larval or juvenile insect stages feed upon. White turtlehead (*Chelone glabra*) is a great example of the importance of host plants, as it is one of the only plant species upon which the Baltimore checkerspot lays its eggs. A gardener interested in attracting this somewhat rare yet exquisite little butterfly would do well to design a garden around turtlehead. Fortunately, it also is a fabulous garden plant, especially for wet soils.

A moderately sized, upright perennial, white turtlehead features interestingly shaped white flowers that resemble a turtle popping its head out of its shell. A related species, pink turtlehead (*C. lyonii*) is far better known and more widely used in gardens than white turtlehead; however, it is not native to New England. Its natural range is far to our south, primarily in North Carolina and Tennessee.

Bumblebees are about the only insects strong enough to force themselves into the flower looking for nectar, and can be found in abundance on white turtlehead. Sun to part shade, average to moist soils, zones 3–9.

White turtlehead is the primary host plant for Baltimore checkerspot caterpillars.

Spring beauty, *Claytonia caroliniana* and *Claytonia virginica*

Nothing cries out, "Spring is finally here!" quite like spring beauty, one of the earliest-flowering spring ephemerals to grace New England gardens. Carolina and Virginia spring beauty are similar in stature, growing to about six inches tall, although *Claytonia caroliniana* has slightly darker flowers and slightly wider leaves than *C. virginica*. Both plants are native throughout much of New England and can be found naturally inhabiting rich, deciduous forests.

In the garden, spring beauty is both a welcome sight for gardeners and an important early nectar source for native bees. Like many ephemeral species, spring beauty can be hard to find available for sale, but it easily spreads itself around the garden if allowed to go to seed. Because it's actively growing only from late March through mid-May, spring beauty can withstand dry soils during its summer dormancy. Part sun to shade, moist spring soils, zones 3–9.

Carolina spring beauty

Spring Ephemerals

Some of the most rewarding native plants to use in the garden are ephemerals like spring beauty and Dutchman's breeches (*Dicentra cucullaria*). These are plants that emerge in early spring, just after (and sometimes during) snowmelt. They are quick to appear, quick to flower, and quick to go dormant, but when naturalized in a garden, they provide a welcome burst of early color after a long, cold winter. While many of them are not particularly difficult to grow, they can be difficult to find available for sale because many nurseries do not have the patience required to grow them. It's best to plant a few and let them go to seed each year, allowing them to naturalize and form large patches over time.

One of the other challenging aspects of using spring ephemerals is the fact that they go dormant after flowering. To use them effectively in the garden without leaving a gaping hole, it's best to interplant them with good companion plants that can complement their spring display with late season interest. Ferns like long beech fern (*Phegopteris connectilis*) work well in this role.

Squirrel corn, *Dicentra canadensis*, and Dutchman's breeches, *Dicentra cucullaria*

Most gardeners are familiar with the common garden bleeding heart *Lamprocapnos* (*Dicentra*) *spectabilis*, a species native to Asia, or the wild bleeding heart, *D. eximia*, which is native to the Appalachian region and as far north as Pennsylvania. Few people are familiar with our two native bleeding hearts, squirrel corn, and Dutchman's breeches (*D. cucullaria*).

Both squirrel corn and Dutchman's breeches are considered true ephemeral species. They emerge in early spring, put on a quick but robust floral display, then quickly develop seed and go dormant, completing their life cycle before the oaks have even leafed out fully in New England. From an ornamental perspective, one of the best advantages to using either of these species in a shade garden is that they enter dormancy quickly, rapidly shedding their spent foliage, which disappears without a long, drawn-out period of yellowing.

Dutchman's breeches flower about a week before squirrel corn. The foliage has a light blue-green cast to it and is finely divided. Once the plants begin to spread around, the foliage itself can add wonderful texture to the garden in early spring. The flowers are pure white and are said to resemble a Dutchman's breeches. Before the flowers of Dutchman's breeches start to fade, squirrel corn begins to bloom. It is named for its corm, which is small, round, bright yellow, and could easily be mistaken for a kernel of corn at first glance. The flower is more like that of the traditional bleeding hearts, though, like Dutchman's breeches, it is pure white.

Squirrel corn has a tendency to spread a little more quickly than Dutchman's breeches, and for this reason, it tends to be our first choice for the garden. But it's rare to find a place at Garden in the Woods with one species and not the other, if for no other reason than because, planted in combination, they offer quite a long, staggered bloom period. Part sun to shade, moist spring soils, zones 3–8.

Dutchman's breeches

Flowering spurge, *Euphorbia corollata*

Fall color is one of the signature elements of the New England land-scape. From sugar maple to highbush blueberry, native trees and shrubs are celebrated across the region for the great burst of color they provide before the cold of winter. But, when designing a garden around fall color, gardeners often overlook the color that herbaceous perennials can contribute. Flowering spurge (*Euphorbia corollata*), a relative of the classic Christmas poinsettia, is by far one of the most stunning perennials for fall color. Brilliant red to orange foliage lasts for several weeks in late fall when many other perennials have gone to bed for winter.

For such a delicate-looking plant, flowering spurge is rather tough, withstanding severely dry soils and full sun. Its wispy form, with clusters of small white flowers at the tips of its stems in midsummer, is a welcome complement to some of the more robust, large perennials that flower at about the same time, like milkweed, aster, ironweed, or Joe-Pye weed.

Flowering spurge

The fall color of flowering spurge

Flowering spurge is fairly slow growing, but will form a sparse, open patch over time that works well when planted in combination with other perennials that can tolerate similar conditions, such as spotted beebalm (*Monarda punctata*), bird's foot violet (*Viola pedata*), and pussytoes (*Antennaria* spp.). The flowers of flowering spurge last for ages before maturing into small green fruits that begin to turn red at the same time as the foliage. An established patch of flowering spurge in October is breathtaking. Sun to part shade, dry soils, zones 3–9.

The purple flowers of spotted Joe-Pye weed contrast nicely with tall yellow flowering perennials like wingstem.

Joe-Pye weed, *Eutrochium (Eupatorium)* spp.

Joe-Pye weed (*Eutrochium* spp.) is a tried and true perennial that many veteran gardeners (native enthusiast or not) have likely worked with before. When grown in dry or shady sites, Joe-Pye weed often tops out around four feet tall, but when given sunny, moist conditions, it will often grow six or even eight feet tall (or taller). Because of its size, many gardeners prefer to plant one of the many dwarf cultivars available on the market. Rather than choosing a cultivar—a genetic clone of all other plants of the same name on the market—we recommend some perennial pruning. A single cutback, when properly timed around the first of June, ensures that your plants will top out around four feet tall and still flower reliably. Indeed, this is a nice technique to use to get plants of differing heights in the garden. Cut some a little earlier or a little later, some a little taller or a little shorter, and create an interesting late season display of Joe-Pye weed of varying heights, all in bloom at the same time.

Flowers range from a bronzy red-pink to a lighter, almost white-pink. If uncut, each stem is topped with a single large inflorescence, but when cut the stems usually branch, and you're more likely to see three to five medium-size clusters of flowers rather than one large flower cluster. Joe-Pye weed lends great structure to the late season garden, providing a large vertical element, with flowers that rise above the rest of a perennial border in late season. They make a great backdrop for smaller perennials or can play the role of tall accents within a mixed meadow or border. If you have a sunny moist area, a combination of Joe-Pye weed, New York ironweed (*Vernonia noveboracensis*), and Turk's cap lily (*Lilium superbum*) makes for a stunning display.

There are four species of Joe-Pye weed native to New England. Of these, hollow Joe-Pye weed (*E. fistulosum*) is the most ornamental, with smaller foliage than that of coastal plain Joe-Pye weed (*E. dubium*), spotted Joe-Pye weed (*E. maculatum*), or purple Joe-Pye weed (*E. purpureum*), though all are great garden plants. Sun to part shade, average to moist soils, zones 3–9.

Common wild strawberry, *Fragaria virginiana*, and woodland strawberry, *Fragaria vesca*

Wild strawberry is high in the running for the most useful native plant in this book. While they are not the showiest ornamentals, nor the tastiest edibles, the two species of wild strawberry here have great potential as garden plants, either as a specimen, in the case of woodland strawberry, or as a replacement for the typical American lawn, in the case of common wild strawberry. Lawns cover nearly 2 percent of the land in the United States, more than forty million acres. Every square inch of it displaces diverse habitat for wildlife and requires maintenance with irrigation, fertilizers, pesticides, and fossil fuel–burning equipment. Despite names like Kentucky bluegrass (*Poa pratensis*), turfgrass species themselves are anything but American, and it's time we really started replacing our lawns with something more sustainable. Wild strawberry represents a good alternative, thriving with little to no maintenance—no water, no fertilizer, and no mowing. At the same time, wild strawberry provides food for people, as well as habitat for countless pollinators.

Common wild strawberry (*Fragaria virginiana*) will spread as far as it is allowed. Its vigor makes it hard to contain in typical garden settings, but because of its quick-spreading habit, it is an ideal lawn alternative. Its leaves play host to dozens of beneficial insects, more than any other native herbaceous plant not named goldenrod or aster. The flowers, which typically appear in mid- to late spring, are pollinated by bees. After pollination, common wild strawberry produces a small, bright red strawberry, no more than an inch in length. Despite its small size, the flavor of common wild strawberry is an incredible combination of sweet and tart that easily puts the big, beautiful supermarket strawberries to shame. At Garden in the Woods, we feature a common wild strawberry lawn in our orchard, where it consistently flowers and fruits every year, just in time for the summer solstice. Sun to part shade, dry to average soils, zones 3–9.

A related species, woodland strawberry (*F. vesca*), is very similar to the plant described above. Like common wild strawberry, woodland strawberry grows well in sun, but also will handle a fair amount of shade. Woodland strawberry is also a better-behaved garden plant, less rambunctious, with more of a clumping than spreading habit, and a sweeter berry. Neither of these strawberries is susceptible to the fungal blight that affects the common garden strawberry. Sun to part shade, dry to average soils, zones 3–9.

Wild strawberry is a great alternative to traditional turfgrass lawns.

Few people stop to appreciate the delicate fruits of wild geranium in summer.

Wild geranium, *Geranium maculatum*

Usually when gardeners hear "geranium," they tend to think of the annual plants (*Pelargonium* × *hortorum*) common in any nursery that sells annual bedding plants. When native plant enthusiasts hear geranium, we tend to think of the tough, reliable perennial *Geranium maculatum*, often simply referred to as wild geranium or sometimes as spotted crane's-bill. This is a tried-and-true garden plant that is easily at home on shady trailsides or in the woodland garden. Pink to purple (occasionally white) flowers appear in late summer and bloom through early fall.

Wild geranium is happiest growing in moist soil, but is also surprisingly drought tolerant. Spring flowers, normally pink, but occasionally white as indicated above, are followed by some very attractive, almost sculptural dry fruit. Fruit develops as tall narrow spikes with the seed held toward the base. As the fruit matures, it dries out, eventually releasing the seed and forcibly shooting it from a swing arm of sorts. It's a stroke of very good luck to actually see this happen, but if not, the evidence remains as the fruit changes from an upright spike to a shape that resembles a chandelier. Sun to part shade, average to moist soils, zones 3–9.

Barren strawberry, *Geum* (*Waldsteinia*) *fragarioides*

Mat-forming evergreen perennials that grow in a wide range of cultural conditions are a panacea for gardeners. Versatile little plants like these are worth their weight in gold for all the function and beauty they provide in a garden. Once established, a dense mat of evergreen perennial foliage provides all the benefits of good mulch—weed suppression, moisture retention, soil protection, and temperature moderation—without requiring the gardener to buy and/or spread it every season.

Barren strawberry (*Geum fragarioides*), one of these valuable little garden heroes, provides some interest for every season in the New England garden. Its bright yellow, mid-spring blossoms resemble the white flowers of its cousin, the wild strawberry. Its evergreen foliage, which also resembles that of strawberries, has a glossy sheen and turns red-purple to bronze in winter.

Perhaps the plant's best attribute is its tolerance of a wide range of cultural conditions. From dry to moist, sun to shade, barren strawberry seems happy no matter where it's growing. Plant it in combination with tall ferns for a nice foliage contrast or beneath shrubs with a sparse habit like mountain laurel (*Kalmia latifolia*). Once established, barren strawberry's dense foliage mat will prevent all but the most vigorous of perennials from growing through it, so plant it cautiously around other species. Sun to shade, average to dry soils, zones 3–8.

Barren strawberry

Bowman's root, *Gillenia trifoliata*

Bowman's root (*Gillenia trifoliata*) is one of those plants that seems to thrive on neglect. It's planted throughout Garden in the Woods in various cultural conditions, from sun to shade, dry to moist, and yet none of our specimens are quite as nice as the patch that planted itself in our front parking lot island. That patch gets run over by a car at least once a year, grows in poor soils with no irrigation, and looks great.

Bowman's root
PHOTO BY AMY NYMAN

Bowman's root should be planted in an open area where the gardener can enjoy and appreciate its open, airy form and thin-petaled white flowers. Its display in a light breeze is wonderful. The movement of its flowers in the wind is reminiscent of the leaves of quaking aspen (*Populus tremuloides*). When not in bloom, Bowman's root's foliage is texturally interesting, with sharp teeth on trifoliate leaves.

Perhaps the best reason to grow bowman's root is for its fall foliage. Like flowering spurge, Bowman's root balks at the rule that says herbaceous perennials don't provide good fall color. Especially when given good sunlight, its fall color runs from bright red to deep maroon, bordering on purple, and lasts for several weeks in September and into October. Sun to part shade, moist to dry soils, zones 4–9.

Jerusalem artichoke, *Helianthus tuberosus*, and woodland sunflower, *Helianthus divaricatus*

Plants in the genus *Helianthus* easily provide some of the best support for beneficial insects and wildlife. Despite the showy yellow flowers much loved by bees, the real value of these plants is as host plants for myriad native butterfly and moth species.

The name sunflower normally conjures images in our minds of the common annual sunflower (*H. annuus*). Though native to the United States, this species is not native to the East Coast. In New England, we find a number of perennial native sunflowers and one whose native range is somewhat controversial.

Jerusalem artichoke or sunchoke (*H. tuberosus*) is controversial in the sense that its introduction to New England was not by natural migration but assisted migration by Native Americans. By the definition provided in the introductory chapters of this book, Jerusalem artichoke certainly can be considered native, having been introduced to New England prior to European settlement. Though incredibly beautiful, Jerusalem artichoke is usually considered more edible than ornamental due to its vigor and flavor. The tubers (fleshy, belowground storage organs like potatoes) taste something like a cross between an artichoke and a potato and are excellent roasted, boiled, fried, or really cooked any way you wish; unfortunately, they also contain an indigestible carbohydrate called inulin that can cause flatulence. As a landscape plant, Jerusalem artichoke is a good choice for a tall, showy, but aggressive plant to use as competitive pressure against invasive plants like Japanese knotweed (*Fallopia japonica*) or common reed (*Phragmites australis*). Sun to part shade, average to moist soils, zones 3–9.

Woodland sunflower (*H. divaricatus*) is not quite as aggressive as Jerusalem artichoke. Though not edible, it is an absolutely beautiful garden plant. Usually growing to about the two- to four-foot range (closer to two feet in dry soils and four feet in moist soils), woodland sunflower is covered in bright yellow flowers in midsummer that are an absolute magnet for bees. Though common in the partial shade of woodland

Jerusalem artichoke tubers are incredibly tasty.

edges, woodland sunflower is just as happy in full sun, and once established will handle drought better than many other native sunflowers. Sun to part sun, average to moist soils, zones 3–9.

Bluets are a great addition to any garden, no matter the size.

Bluets, *Houstonia caerulea*

Bluets (*Houstonia caerulea*) are small enough to fit into the smallest crack in a stone patio and yet showy enough that no garden should be without them. Usually about three inches tall, bluets have flowers that can be three-quarters of an inch across and almost seem like they should belong to a much larger plant. Basal foliage gives rise to narrow flowering stems with flowers that range in color from white to pale blue with a bright yellow center. Bluets work well planted along trail edges, or anywhere they can grow in between rocks or in old tree stumps. Many a garden designer has built a patio with stones that were purposely spaced apart just enough to allow bluets to be sown in between them. The resulting landscape feature is beautiful, with hundreds of bluets popping up between the rock crevices, topped in white to blue flowers each spring.

Bluets bloom most heavily in spring and early summer and then sporadically through summer and into fall. At Garden in the Woods, where we have spent the last several years spreading bluets throughout the garden, there is barely a time from spring to fall when there aren't a few bluets in flower. Bluets spread themselves around by seed somewhat prolifically, although they tend to seed themselves into poor soils and trail edges, where we consider them welcome additions rather than weeds. When we find them growing in a spot where we don't want them, we delicately dig them out for planting in other areas. This plant is incredibly easy to grow from seed. After flowering, bluet seed ripens and is ready to collect in midsummer when the fruits dry and turn brown. Seed can simply be spread onto bare soil in the garden and new plants will often emerge about a month later. Sun to part shade, dry to moist soils, zones 3–9.

Blue flag iris, *Iris versicolor*

With a distinct upright habit and a striking purple to blue flower, there is no mistaking blue flag iris (*Iris versicolor*) in the garden. In mid-spring, when blue flag iris begins to send up new foliage, it often emerges with a distinct purple coloration that quickly fades to green as the purple pigment (anthocyanin) dissipates in its leaves in favor of green pigment (chlorophyll). Its leaves are roughly an inch wide and stand straight up, providing an attractive, clean, vertical accent in the garden even when the flowers are not in bloom. Blue flag iris works well in combination with other plants that grow in similar habitats like rose milkweed (*Asclepias incarnata*), or low groundcovers like running groundsel (*Packera obovata*).

Blue flag iris flowers are incredible—often purple though sometimes blue and with varying degrees of white and yellow mottling. Occasionally, a plant will display pure white flowers, and mixing a combination of purple, blue, and white always puts on a spectacular show.

Though happiest in moist to wet sites, even growing occasionally in standing water, blue flag iris also grows quite well in average garden soils. They seem to have a heavier floral display when planted in wet soils, but an old patch in the propagation beds at Garden in the Woods continues to thrive in a fairly dry site. Sun to part shade, moist soils, zones 4–9.

Blue flag iris

Twinleaf, *Jeffersonia diphylla*

Contrary to popular opinion, twinleaf (*Jeffersonia diphylla*) is not a spring ephemeral. Although most plant catalogs and gardening books place it into this category, it's a better foliage plant than most anything. In fact, we think twinleaf should be considered as a great native plant replacement for hosta in the shade garden.

Its flowers are indeed beautiful . . . for all of about thirty minutes in a typical spring. There are occasions, when the temperature is just right, when twinleaf flowers might last for several days, but they are fleeting at best, and growing them for their flowers is a sure way to get frustrated with this plant.

The foliage is what really sets this plant apart. While the flowers may not last long, the foliage sure does, lasting and looking great well into fall. The leaves lend the plant its common name, being divided into two sections that resemble the ears of an elephant, or the wings of an angel. The individual leaves grow wider and wider as the season progresses and

Twinleaf

The interesting fruits of twinleaf

are a nice blue-green. The bold foliage contrasts wonderfully with finer-leaved plants like lady fern (*Athyrium angustum*), Canada mayflower (*Maianthemum canadense*), or Pennsylvania sedge (*Carex pensylvanica*).

Though also short lived, the fruits of twinleaf are quite interesting. They are not pretty as much as they are fascinating, almost resembling a small green trash can with a hinged lid. As the fruit matures, it fades from green to yellow, drying until the top pops open and dumps its seeds onto the ground. Each deep brown seed has an attached elaiosome, a fleshy attachment rich in lipids, which attracts ants that will quickly gather up the seeds and carry them back to their burrows. By dragging the twinleaf seeds around, ants help distribute them throughout the garden, where you'll find them as seedlings several years later. Part shade to shade, average to moist soils, zones 4–9.

Cardinal flower, *Lobelia cardinalis*, and blue lobelia, *Lobelia siphilitica*

Though there are six native species in the genus *Lobelia*, there are really only two that are regularly used in gardens—cardinal flower (*L. cardinalis*) and blue lobelia (*L. siphilitica*). Cardinal flower is the better known of the two species, and is commonly recognized to be a great hummingbird attractant. With its vibrant red flowers, it is not difficult to see why hummingbirds find it so appealing. Cardinal flower also is a good example of how flower shape can indicate "who" might be responsible for pollinating a flowering plant. In this case, cardinal flowers have a deep, tubular shape; only a hummingbird, with its long beak, or a butterfly with a long proboscis (tongue) can reach the nectar at the bottom of the tube. Sun to part sun, moist to wet soils, zones 3–9.

Blue lobelia was once touted as a cure for syphilis, hence the botanical name *L. siphilitica*. It was so well-known for its curative properties that during colonial times it was widely collected and shipped back to the Old World to help those in need. Unfortunately for them, it has absolutely no effect on syphilis. Despite its shortcomings as a medicinal plant, blue lobelia does have some great ornamental attributes, including a true blue flower. Ignoring the color difference between the flowers of blue lobelia and cardinal flower, you'll notice that blue lobelia flowers are broader and stouter. This shape not only gives bees a place to land, but it also is one of the key indicators this plant is pollinated by bees. Sun, moist to wet soils, zones 3–9.

Recent research at the University of Vermont demonstrated the potentially harmful impact that plant breeding can have on pollinators and other beneficial insects. Comparing the nectar quality of several common cardinal flower and blue lobelia hybrids, Annie White, PhD, was able to demonstrate that hybridization sometimes leads to plants with the physical attributes of one parent, yet lacking the appropriate sugar content in their nectar to support those organisms that are attracted to the flower. For example, *L.* × *speciosa* 'Fan Scarlet,' a commonly sold hybrid cultivar of these two species, resembles cardinal flower, yet has just 20 percent of the nectar energy of the natural species.

Those gardeners interested in attracting hummingbirds to their gardens should avoid hybrids and cultivars in favor of natural species to ensure their gardens best support the pollinators they attract.

Plant both cardinal flower and blue lobelia in areas where you can create some soil disturbance every year. Both plants are short lived but spread easily from seed, providing that seed can find some bare soil. In the wild, disturbance often occurs on streambanks or where animals dig. In the garden, we sometimes see lobelias growing around newly planted trees in areas where we haven't seen a lobelia plant in years.

Cardinal flower

Sundial lupine

Sundial lupine, *Lupinus perennis*

Sundial lupine (*Lupinus perennis*) is happiest in sunny, sandy sites and is as good a choice for open meadows as it is for roadsides and other sites with poor, dry soils. The plant features intricate, compound leaves that provide wonderful texture both before and after the flowers bloom. Sundial lupine has a tendency to capture droplets of rain and dew on its foliage, making it a garden photographer's dream.

Purple to blue flowers open in late spring, followed by pea-like pods in summer. Between the palmate leaves and the upright flower spikes, lupine has a dramatic impact in the ornamental garden. It works well as a vertical accent among shorter plants like bearberry (*Arctostaphylos uva-ursi*) or eastern prickly pear (*Opuntia humifusa*), but can also work well as filler, occupying the empty space among larger clumping grasses or taller, late season perennials like yellow wild indigo (*Baptisia tinctoria*).

Sundial lupine is the only host plant for the Karner blue butterfly, a federally endangered insect and the state butterfly of New Hampshire, where its only remaining populations in New England can be found. Unfortunately, when shopping for lupines in many garden centers, the only plant available for sale is the western lupine (*L. polyphyllus*), an introduced species from the West Coast of the United States. Though they make attractive garden plants, research has demonstrated that, while adult Karner blue butterflies will lay eggs on western lupine, their caterpillars are unable to feed on the plants and subsequently die. Sundial lupine is a prime example of a plant that plays a vital ecological role. The only reason the Karner blue butterfly is endangered is loss of habitat, in this case, the decline of sundial lupine. The only way to bring the Karner blue butterfly back from the brink of extinction is to restore the sundial lupine. Sun, dry to average soils, zones 3–9.

Solomon's plume, *Maianthemum racemosum*, and Canada mayflower, *Maianthemum canadense*

The genus *Maianthemum* now includes plants that previously resided in the genus *Smilacina*, including Solomon's plume (*M. racemosum*) and starry false Solomon's seal (*M. stellatum*). Both are great garden plants, although they can be difficult to find available for sale. Solomon's plume, also known as false Solomon's seal, is often overlooked and underappreciated. In the wild, it forms loose patches with consistent albeit small flowers and a semiconsistent fruit set. When brought into the garden, Solomon's plume can grow to a thick, tight clump with large, plume-like flowers followed by bright red, edible berries. For such a showy species, it is difficult to imagine why it is not a more popular garden plant. Solomon's plume

Canada mayflower
PHOTO BY JACKIE DONNELLY

The edible fruits of Solomon's plume

is tolerant of a range of moisture conditions, and it can do well in that impossible mix of dry soil and dense shade. The one potential downside to Solomon's plume is that it can be a touch slow to establish in the garden. Part shade to shade, average to moist soils, zones 3–8.

Canada mayflower (*M. canadense*), like Solomon's plume, is also an underappreciated garden plant, though in a different way. Most people who are at least peripherally familiar with it claim that it is weedy and not showy enough for garden use. While it is a fast spreader and can be moderately aggressive, those attributes make it an ideal living mulch. Canada mayflower also happens to be quite shallow rooted, making it perfectly suited to interplant with just about any tall, shade-loving clumping plant. Canada mayflower resembles the non-native lily-of-the-valley (*Convallaria majalis*), which is most certainly more vigorous in habit. When given a little sun and decent soil, Canada mayflower will have a much more consistent bloom and fruit set, making it quite an attractive garden plant for tough places. Part shade to shade, dry to moist soils, zones 3–8.

Virginia bluebells, *Mertensia virginica*

Virginia bluebells (*Mertensia virginica*) are always a welcome sign that spring has truly arrived in the Northeast, flowering in late April to early May, just before what one might consider peak bloom time in New England. Like many other ephemeral species, Virginia bluebells prefers to grow in the dappled shade and rich organic soils of a deciduous forest, but it also is fairly versatile. We often find ourselves weeding this plant out of gravel pathways, where it seems to grow quite well.

The emerging foliage almost looks like lettuce starts—purple to bright green and oblong—until the flower stalks begin to develop. Bluebells flowers open from pink-purple buds to reveal true blue flowers, a rarity in plants. The flowers continue to bloom for a few weeks in early to mid-spring, before both flowers and foliage start to fade. By midsummer, most of its leaves have yellowed and started to die back as it goes dormant until next spring.

Because Virginia bluebells is a true spring ephemeral, people have a difficult time understanding how to use it effectively in a garden. If not planted in combination with later season perennials, ephemerals can leave large holes in the garden once dormant. But with a little planning, later season perennials like bugbane (*Actaea racemosa*), Solomon's plume (*Maianthemum racemosum*), and American spikenard (*Aralia racemosa*) will emerge after Virginia bluebells' flower display and then mask the fading foliage as it goes dormant. You can never have too many ephemerals! Think about areas in your garden where you could use a bit more early season color, and even if you have established perennials planted there already, you can plant ephemerals like Virginia bluebells right in among them.

Combine Virginia bluebells with wood poppies (*Stylophorum diphyllum*) and foamflower (*Tiarella cordifolia* var. *cordifolia*) for an easy, "bulletproof" display that will carry your garden from early to late spring. Throw in some King Solomon's seal (*Polygonatum biflorum*) and bugbane (*Actaea racemosa*), add water and compost, and enjoy your new shade garden. Part shade to shade, average soils, moist in spring, zones 3–9.

Virginia bluebells

Beebalm, *Monarda* spp.

The New England ecoregions are home to four native beebalm (*Monarda*) species. The common scarlet beebalm (*M. didyma*) is probably the most well-known of the four, and though technically native, it is only just so. Scarlet beebalm thrives in moist meadows but will struggle in drier sites and suffers badly from powdery mildew when not in moist enough soils. Despite all the powdery mildew–resistant cultivars available, the best option to avoid this garden malady is to plant scarlet beebalm in the right place. When grown in full sun with moist soils, scarlet beebalm is stunning. The leaves and flowers are edible and make a very flavorful tea (or mojito); hence it's secondary common name, Oswego tea. Sun to part shade, average to moist soils, zones 3–9.

Wild bergamot (*M. fistulosa*) is native across the region, occurring naturally in all six New England states. The flower varies from pink to purple and is most often a shade of periwinkle. While wild bergamot prefers moist meadows, it's much more tolerant of drought than scarlet beebalm. Also edible, this plant has a bit more of an herbal flavor, something like a combination of basil and citrus. The story goes that when the colonists got angry enough at the British to dump all the tea in the Boston Harbor, they needed a good replacement for imported tea. A combination of wild bergamot and New Jersey tea (*Ceanothus americanus*) made a very decent replacement, and tastes remarkably like Earl Grey. Sun to part shade, average to moist soils, zones 3–8.

Spotted beebalm (*M. punctata*) looks like something out of a Dr. Seuss book, and unlike the prior two species, this one thrives in poor, dry, sandy soils. A short-lived species, each individual plant usually lives for just two to four years; however, it self-sows regularly, and if allowed to drop its seed, spotted beebalm can form long-lived populations in the garden. For this species (as well as all the other *Monarda* species, and for the most part just about all the species in this book), we don't recommend deadheading unless you specifically want to control the spread of this plant. Not only does the developing seed ensure the long-term survival of the plant in your garden, but it also is excellent birdseed for fall and winter foragers. Why clean up your garden in the fall only to go to the store and buy birdseed when your garden can provide that seed (and good winter protection) free of charge and with less work than the fall cleanup usually takes? Sun to part shade, dry to average soils, zones 4–9.

A goldenrod crab spider captures a bumblebee on spotted beebalm.

Running groundsel, *Packera obovata*, and golden groundsel, *Packera aurea*

There are four species of *Packera* in New England, two of which we highly recommend for garden use. Of the two, running groundsel (*P. obovata*) is more garden-worthy. Perhaps more beautiful before it starts to flower than while in flower, running groundsel has incredible early spring emergence, when bright, glossy green foliage with a purple tint begins to emerge. The underside of its leaves is purple throughout the season, while the upper leaf surfaces range from mostly green to mostly purple. This coloration holds as the flower buds begin to stretch up, reaching about ten inches tall.

The flower buds themselves are the same purple as the leaf underside, and until you get to know the plant, you'd guess that a purple flower will soon emerge. But as the buds begin to open, very narrow yellow petals appear, surrounding a purple center. As the petals widen, the purple center fades to yellow until there is no evidence of the purple

Running groundsel

color left. Around the same time, the purple starts to fade from the upper leaf surfaces, leaving a deep, glossy green that plays off the bright yellow of the flowers beautifully. The foliage ranges from deeply lobed on the floral stems to entire and toothed at the base and, with the gloss present, remains interesting all season long.

Running groundsel is a spreading species that can move rather quickly, especially when given sunny, moist conditions. It stays low, rarely getting much higher than two inches (not including the flower stems), and works well when interplanted with taller accent plants. Running groundsel also works well planted in a tall meadow, where its evergreen foliage and early spring color provide interest in a planting with mostly late season interest. Although it doesn't die to the ground like ephemerals, it can tolerate the shade cast by tall grasses and other perennials later in the season. Full sun to part shade, average to wet soils, zones 3–8.

Golden groundsel (*P. aurea*) is a touch slower growing than running groundsel, but what it lacks in speed, it makes up for in size. Unlike its lower-growing cousin, golden groundsel gets quite large and works better as an accent than a groundcover. Because it is a rather robust plant, it should not be planted around more delicate perennials. Its flowers are almost identical to running groundsel, but its foliage lacks any purple coloration. Full sun to part shade, average to wet soils, zones 3–8.

Garden phlox, *Phlox* spp.

Phlox (*Phlox* spp.) is a versatile genus, with plants well adapted to a variety of cultural conditions. From wild blue phlox with its fragrant mid-spring flowers to common garden phlox with its midsummer flowers, there is a phlox for just about any season and any place in the garden.

Starting in the sun, we find moss phlox (*P. subulata*), named for its minute leaves and low growth habit, which combine to give it a moss-like appearance when not in bloom. Flowering occurs in early spring and is often so robust that the leaves are hidden entirely. Moss phlox is a well-known rock garden plant, as it grows best in full sun and well-drained soils. When placed on top of a retaining wall or a boulder, moss phlox can climb over or hang down, softening otherwise hard landscape features and providing a beautiful, soft carpet. The foliage is quite short, and even when in bloom, if this plant appears six inches tall, it's because it's growing on top of a five-inch rock.

Wild blue phlox pairs wonderfully with a variety of spring-blooming native species.

Common garden phlox (*Phlox paniculata*) is the phlox with which most people are acquainted. Usually referred to simply as garden phlox, this plant does best when grown in sunny, moist soils, and though it's capable of growing in some shade or in drier sites, it will suffer badly from powdery mildew when unhappy. There are enumerable mildew-resistant cultivars on the market, though none of them will provide more powdery mildew resistance than a garden phlox simply planted in the right spot. Sun to part shade, average to moist soils, zones 4–8.

Easily one of the best plants for a shade garden is wild blue phlox (*P. divaricata*). It does best in part sun to shade and prefers rich soils when it can get them, but is drought tolerant once established. Color forms range from white to pink to blue-purple, but the real reason to plant wild blue phlox is for its fragrance. It's sweet, yet delicate, and is one of the finest fragrant flowers to bloom in spring. Combined with running foamflower (*Tiarella cordifolia* var. *cordifolia*), wild blue phlox puts on an impressive spring display for your eyes and your sense of smell! Part shade to shade, average to moist soils, zones 3–9.

Mayapple, *Podophyllum peltatum*

Mayapple (*P. peltatum*) is often thought of as a garden thug. It has certainly earned this reputation, as it is quite vigorous and shades out all but the most vigorous of other perennials. This is not a delicate plant for a small space, but in the right place, it can be a rather effective design element. Like many other spreading plants, choosing the right location for mayapple can mean the difference between an extremely useful plant and a maintenance nightmare. In the right place, mayapple is an attractive groundcover in spring to summer.

Mayapple emerges in early spring looking a bit like a green lollipop. The leaves appear to almost corkscrew out of the ground, tightly bound at first before unfurling to reveal a large, umbrella-shaped leaf. In terms of ornamental attractiveness, mayapple's early spring emergence is certainly its most attractive quality. The textures are fabulous and are usually accentuated by varying degrees of red and purple leaf mottling.

Mayapple in early spring

Soon after the foliage has fully opened, fragrant white flowers open beneath the leaves. The leaf obscures the flower, masking it from the viewer unless the leaves are brushed aside. A good trick to avoid this and reveal the flower is to plant mayapple on a steep slope, where you can admire its flower from below. When looking down from above, the thick foliage provides great texture in the garden; when looking up from below, all the flowers are visible. After the flowers pass, the "apples" begin to form. Though not every plant will produce a fruit, once you have a small patch of them, you'll have enough to enjoy. They are dispersed by box turtles (among other animals), though we recommend eating a few yourself, as they have a distinct flavor that can only be described as mayapple-like.

Mayapple does move around in the garden, especially when grown in part shade and moist soils. Plant it only where you want more of it, and intermix it with plants that have late season character, as mayapple is ephemeral in nature. By mid- to late summer, the foliage will have gone dormant. Part shade to shade, average to moist soils, zones 3–9.

King Solomon's seal, *Polygonatum biflorum*

King Solomon's seal (*Polygonatum biflorum*) has some amazing attributes and some qualities that tend to drive people nuts, as well as one benefit we almost never hear mentioned. King Solomon's seal's arching branches grow typically anywhere from about eighteen to thirty inches tall, and occasionally up to about forty-eight inches. The leaves attach directly to the stem and have a zipper-like zigzag character.

Bell-shaped flowers dangle from beneath the stems in spring, and are quite visible despite their placement below the foliage. Bees absolutely love the flowers; if you're looking for a good way to attract and support bees, then this plant should most certainly appear in your garden. Dark blue fruit follows each flower and at times can outlast the foliage. It is not uncommon late in the season to see a King Solomon's seal stem and its distinctive growth habit with nothing but gorgeous blue berries hanging beneath it. King Solomon's seal is quite tolerant of a range of light conditions, from almost full sun to almost full shade. While it prefers rich soils, it becomes tolerant of drought once established.

From a design perspective, King Solomon's seal can be quite difficult to use because of its two-dimensional growth habit and its tendency to send stems in any and all directions. Proper siting can go a long way toward preventing this issue once you recognize that the stems reach toward light out of the shadows. For this reason, the plant is perhaps best used under trees or on the edges of paths where the stems will reach in the light's direction.

For some reason, very few people think to eat these plants, and those few who do only seem to go for the roots (which taste something like wood ash). The berries are inedible, but the stems are quite tasty when treated in a manner similar to asparagus. Cut stems in the early season when the leaves are still tightly curled. Peel off the leaves and eat the stems either raw or cooked; the flavor is sweet and very "green" (slightly cucumber, slightly asparagus). They can sometimes be mucilaginous when raw, though this texture will dissipate when stems are cooked. Don't miss out on these tasty, shade-tolerant plants! Part shade to shade, average to moist soils, zones 3–9.

King Solomon's seal
PHOTO BY WILLIAM CULLINA

Mountain mint, *Pycnanthemum* spp.

When most gardeners hear "mint" they run away screaming, expecting garden thugs that take over and offer little aesthetic value. But our native flora has some outstanding mints. From the beebalms (*Monarda* spp.) to the hyssops (*Agastache* spp.), there are a variety of better-behaved native mints that are beautiful pollinator magnets. A lesser-known native mint is mountain mint (*Pycnanthemum* spp.). Altogether, there are six native species in New England, as well as some naturally occurring hybrids. While many of them are quite similar from a horticultural point of view, there are a few standouts that make excellent garden plants.

You can generally break the mountain mints into dry-loving or moisture-loving plants. Aesthetically, the most attractive is the moisture-loving, broad-leaved mountain mint (*P. muticum*). Found on pond or stream edges, bottomlands, floodplains, or really anywhere with moist to wet soils and sun, broad-leaved mountain mint is a great plant for supporting myriad pollinators. Its flowers are quite small, although very colorful upon close inspection. The plant makes up for its flower size by producing large, silvery bracts (modified leaves) below the flowers that shine in the sun. The bracts are not only showy on their own, but they also provide a backdrop to show off the small white to pink flowers. Broad-leaved mountain mint can be quite spectacular when in bloom and looks as good in large sweeps as it does as a unique specimen. Combine it with rose milkweed (*Asclepias incarnata*) and New York ironweed (*Vernonia noveboracensis*) next to a large water feature or wet, sunny spot in the garden. Sun to part sun, average to moist soils, zones 3–9.

If you like broad-leaved mountain mint but don't have the right combination of sun and moist soils, then look for hoary mountain mint (*P. incanum*). Its overall aesthetic effect is similar to broad-leaved mountain mint, but its leaves are slightly smaller and covered in fine hairs. Both hoary mountain mint and narrow-leaved mountain mint (*P. tenuifolium*) thrive in drier sites and work well in combination with other dry-loving species like butterfly milkweed (*Asclepias tuberosa*) and stiff aster (*Ionactis linariifolia*). The leaves of narrow-leaved mountain mint are almost needle-like in appearance, and while it lacks the showy bracts of the other two species, its flower is more attractive and produced in more abundance. Each of the mountain mints is a true pollinator magnet. Brush up against them to enjoy their mild, spicy fragrance. Sun to part sun, average to dry soils, zones 3–9.

Broad-leaved mountain mint

Black-eyed Susan, *Rudbeckia* spp.

Black-eyed Susans (*Rudbeckia* spp.) are old standbys in the garden, and for good reason. They thrive in some of the toughest New England seasons and yet continue to produce large, showy flowers at a time of year when many other plants have either finished flowering or have yet to begin.

Showy coneflower (*R. fulgida*) is the most commonly used garden plant in this genus. A consistent perennial, showy coneflower thrives in sunny, dry sites, where it produces long-lasting clusters of bright yellow flowers with a dark eye. Usually growing up to three feet tall, showy coneflower is larger than common black-eyed Susan (*R. hirta*), but quite a bit smaller than cutleaf coneflower (*R. laciniata*). Sun to part shade, average to moist soils, zones 3–9.

While showy coneflower is perhaps the most commonly used garden plant, common black-eyed Susan is our personal favorite. *R. hirta* is a biennial, or short-lived, perennial that produces an abundance of

Common black-eyed Susan

seed; for this reason, it is a fantastic garden plant, especially for those on a budget. If you're looking for a long-lived perennial, one that you can point to for decades and say, "I planted that," then go with showy coneflower. If, on the other hand, you'd like a versatile garden plant that will spread around from seed without any assistance from you, go with common black-eyed Susan. Plant a few or spread some seed in any new planting bed and it will quickly fill in all the voids between other plants in the garden. This technique will not only give you a beautiful garden very quickly, but it will also save you hours of weeding, because the plant will occupy all that otherwise empty space before weeds can get established. As a biennial, common black-eyed Susan is a fast-growing plant that will quickly disappear once other, long-lived perennials fill in, being relegated to those places in your garden where its seed can find some bare soil. If you are planting a garden of any sort in full sun, there is no more functional and useful plant than common black-eyed Susan. It works as a cover crop to keep weeds at bay, retain soil moisture, and give you a huge splash of color all summer. Common black-eyed Susan is incredibly drought tolerant. Sun to part shade, dry to average soils, zones 4–8.

Finally, cutleaf coneflower is a great summer blooming perennial for moist to wet soils. Cutleaf coneflower is quite different from the other two rudbeckias, consistently reaching heights of five to eight feet and preferring moist sites. A large patch of them around the Lily Pond at Garden in the Woods provides masses of smaller yellow flowers in late July through September. The cut leaves lend a unique texture to the garden, and if we had to choose a favorite rudbeckia based on foliage alone, this would be the clear winner. Sun to part shade, average to moist soils, zones 3–9.

Bloodroot

Bloodroot, *Sanguinaria canadensis*

Bloodroot (*Sanguinaria canadensis*) is another great example of a native ephemeral species, and like many of the others, its best characteristics are often overlooked because of our obsession with flowers. The flowers of bloodroot are certainly worth obsessing over—emerging first thing in spring, wrapped in an embrace from a single leaf, which acts like the perfect frame for a garden photographer. The flowers are an absolute pure white, and unlike many other white flowers, they remain white until they drop off the flower instead of yellowing or browning first. The only downside to the flower is its ephemeral nature—for all its beauty, it does not last long enough. There are some double-flower forms that last quite a bit longer, but like many other double flowers, they are sterile and cannot provide nectar or pollen for pollinators, nor can they produce seed to spread themselves around in the garden. A mixture of the natural form and the double form (as well as the occasional pink-flowered form) looks incredible in combination.

Despite the short duration of its flowering season, bloodroot's leaves last for quite a while (it seems to be a reluctant ephemeral species), and this is one of those plants whose leaves are interesting enough to plant just for its foliage alone. Emerging wrapped around the flower bud in very early spring, once the flowers begin to bloom, the individual leaves reveal a nice shade of blue-green. Bloodroot's leaves, perhaps partially because they emerge when the sun is low on the horizon, have a tendency to almost glow when backlit by the sun, wonderfully showing off their intricate venation and unique leaf shape. The leaves are quite large, expanding to at least six or seven inches across, and lend a coarse texture at maturity. Plant it in combination with ferns and small-leaved perennials like wild blue phlox (*Phlox divaricata*) or Canada mayflower (*Maianthemum canadense*) for a fabulous textural display in a shady garden. Part shade to shade, average, well-drained soils, zones 3–9.

Purple pitcher plant, *Sarracenia purpurea*

Like something out of a horror movie, our native pitcher plant (*Sarracenia purpurea*) is completely unique in its adaptations and horticultural intrigue. Naturally occurring in extremely wet, acidic, and nutrient-poor sites, pitcher plants have evolved the ability to acquire nutrients in an unusual way—by digesting insects. They accomplish this amazing feat through insectivorous leaves (produced after flowering so as not to eat their pollinators) in the shape of tall cups filled with fluid, into which they excrete a small arsenal of enzymes that both attract and digest any insect unfortunate enough to make its way inside. As if this adaptation were not impressive enough, the insides of pitcher plant's green to purple leaves are covered in dozens of downward-pointing hairs that are quite easy for an insect to climb down, but impossible to climb back up. Any insect that is unlucky enough to find itself trapped in the fluid of the pitcher will be slowly digested by the enzymatic fluid, providing ample nutrients for this amazing plant.

Purple pitcher plant flowers

The intriguing foliage of purple pitcher plant

In case this insectivorous adaptation is not enough enticement to grow these plants, pitcher plants also produce an exquisite flower in spring. It is quite rare to find a plant that is both an interesting conversation piece for adults and intensely interesting to young children, while providing a splash of unusual beauty in the garden. The flower is deep red in color, with sections of green and yellow mixed in for variety. Avoid the double-flowered cultivars available for sale; too many petals just ruin the plant's elegant architecture. This is not a flower that needed improvement.

While pitcher plants are naturally found growing in acidic bogs, they are surprisingly easy in cultivation. Plant them anywhere that's moist, mildly acidic, and sunny, and they'll be just fine. If you cannot quite find a spot in the garden, they also are easy in containers. Simply plug up the drainage hole with a cork or wax candle; you'll find that although they need moist conditions, they really don't use up much water. Combine them with some sundews (*Drosera* spp.) and a few cranberries (*Vaccinium macrocarpon*) in a container for the perfect bog garden. Sun to part sun, moist to wet soils, zones 2–9.

Wild senna, *Senna hebecarpa*

There are plenty of tall yellow, summer-blooming, drought-tolerant herbaceous perennials in New England, but few have quite as many virtues as wild senna (*Senna hebecarpa*). From an ecological perspective, wild senna attracts and supports more bees than any other plant that blooms at the same time, with flowers that seem almost to have been designed in a lab specifically for bees. In addition to its flowers, wild senna produces nectary glands on its petioles (leaf stems) that feed ants and other visitors before the flowers open, an interesting adaptation. There is speculation that the plant receives benefits from this additional nectar production, in the form of protection offered by ants in return for the food source.

In addition to its ecological value, wild senna is a stunning ornamental plant. Bright yellow flower petals are contrasted by dark (almost black) anthers at their center. Wild senna flowers prolifically on tall, upright stems that stand as high as six feet without any support. Its compound leaves are made up of seven or more leaflets, giving it a soft appearance in stark contrast to its robust stems.

At Garden in the Woods, we regard wild senna as a tough, aggressive plant that borders on garden thug, but it is especially rare in the wild in New England, where it is restricted to moist bottomlands. Wild senna thrives in dry sites and has no problem with drought. As with many tall, summer-blooming species, wild senna is quite vigorous and should only be planted among other vigorous plants that can withstand its competition. Sun to part shade, dry to moist soils, zones 3–9.

Wild senna is a pollinator magnet.

Blue-eyed grass, *Sisyrinchium angustifolium*

Blue-eyed grass (*Sisyrinchium angustifolium*) is not a grass, but an iris relative that offers the same color scheme as blue flag iris (*Iris versicolor*) in a much smaller package. Although in the wild, growing in

Blue-eyed grass
PHOTO BY WILLIAM CULLINA

Native Plants for New England Gardens

competition with taller grasses and perennials, blue-eyed grass can reach as high as eighteen inches, in the garden it typically tops out at about twelve inches. Flower color ranges from true blue to almost purple, with a bright yellow eye that contrasts nicely against the petals. Blue-eyed grass naturally grows in moist meadows and wetland edges, and prefers moist soils; however, once established, it becomes quite drought tolerant. A closely related species, strict blue-eyed grass (*Sisyrinchium montanum*), is a better choice for truly dry sites. The two plants are nearly identical, so much so that some taxonomists consider them to be the same species.

Blue-eyed grass only opens its flowers during the day when the sun hits it, an adaptation that likely contributes to its long-lasting flowers. At Garden in the Woods, we consistently see blue-eyed grass flowering from mid-May through the end of June. Even after its initial flowering period, blue-eyed grass flowers sporadically the rest of the summer. When not in bloom, blue-eyed grass looks a bit like purple lovegrass (*Eragrostis spectabilis*), a common native warm-season grass, making it a good plant to use for testing the plant knowledge of your gardening friends. Sun to part sun, average to moist soils, zones 3–9.

Goldenrod, *Solidago* spp.

Beloved by beekeepers and butterflies, detested by farmers, for whom it's an agricultural weed, and blamed for hay fever by the unknowing, goldenrod (*Solidago* spp.) is a lightning rod that generates equal parts love and hate in New England. With more than twenty-five species in the region, goldenrod is a diverse and important group of plants. For garden purposes, goldenrods range from large, sun-loving perennials that work well in a mixed meadow, to smaller, shade-loving perennials that work well in the late summer garden.

Although it is almost universally blamed for causing hay fever in New England, nothing could be further from the truth. Consider the flowers. Bright yellow and quite showy, goldenrod flowers have one purpose from the plant's perspective: to attract pollinators. Plants with showy flowers almost never cause hay fever because they produce relatively little pollen and their pollen is too heavy to be moved effectively by wind. In this case, the reason goldenrod is so often blamed for causing hay fever is that it blooms at exactly the same time as the real culprit, ragweed (*Ambrosia* spp.). Unlike goldenrod, ragweed produces unremarkable greenish flowers that produce a ton of pollen that is carried from plant to plant by the wind. In late summer and early fall, the air is awash with ragweed pollen and people start to sneeze, but goldenrod is not responsible.

From an ecological perspective, goldenrod is literally the group of herbaceous perennials that supports the highest number of beneficial insects in New England. There are dozens, if not hundreds, of moth and butterfly species whose caterpillars host on goldenrod, and literally hundreds of native bees that feed on goldenrod. The insects that feed on goldenrod are critically important for songbirds, who primarily feed their young a protein-laden diet consisting mainly of larval insects like caterpillars.

For ornamental garden use, there is a goldenrod for just about any situation, from tall, aggressive species that will colonize a meadow, like Canada goldenrod (*S. canadensis*) and wrinkle-leaved goldenrod (*S. rugosa*), to well-behaved choices like downy goldenrod (*S. puberula*).

Wreath goldenrod

Downy goldenrod thrives in sunny, dry sites, and when grown in very sandy sites will often top out at around twelve to eighteen inches tall; when given richer soils, it can top thirty-six inches. Its basal leaves are quite large (four inches long and 1½ inches wide), but the leaves along its stem get smaller, almost to the point of disappearing, toward the top of its flowering stalk. Downy goldenrod is a clumping species that will not dominate the landscape like many of its cousins. Sun to part shade, dry to average soils, zones 2–8.

Wreath goldenrod (*S. caesia*), while happy to grow in sun, is more at home in the shade, where its yellow flowers brighten a shade garden in fall. This plant produces flowers all along its stems instead of at the end of the stem like downy goldenrod. While its blue-tinted foliage is interesting, the flower is the reason to plant wreath goldenrod. Part shade to shade, dry to average soils, zones 3–9.

New England aster and wrinkle-leaved goldenrod

Aster, *Symphyotrichum novae-angliae*, *Ionactis linariifolia*, *Symphyotrichum cordifolium*, and *Eurybia divaricata*

Asters once were all members of the genus *Aster*, but recently they were divided into several different genera, from *Eurybia* to *Symphyotrichum*. Because there are so many asters in New England, they can be found growing from full sun to dense shade, from wet to dry soils, and everything in between. Asters also happen to be one of the most important groups of herbaceous plants for native butterflies and moths, acting as host plants for more caterpillar species than all but the goldenrods (*Solidago* spp.).

Probably the most commonly planted aster in our region is New England aster (*Symphyotrichum novae-angliae*), a tall, sun-loving plant with late season flowers that range from violet-pink to purple. New England aster grows as tall as six feet and prefers moist soils. One of the

Blue wood or heart-leaved aster
PHOTO BY TOM POTTERFIELD

most commonly available cultivars of New England aster is *S. novae-angliae* 'Purple Dome,' a dwarf form (growing only to twenty-four inches) with deep purple flowers. While the shorter stature provides those with smaller gardens an opportunity to use New England aster, the trouble with a form like Purple Dome is that its flower color is much darker than that found on the natural form of New England aster. Recent research has demonstrated that pollinators visit off-color forms of native plants with far less frequency. To best support native bees and other pollinators, it's important to keep this fact in mind and plant more than just cultivars in the garden. Sun to part sun, average to moist soils, zones 3–9.

While New England aster performs best in moist, sunny conditions, stiff aster (*Ionactis linariifolia*) thrives in the driest of sites. Tiny, narrow leaves look almost like the needles of a spruce tree and turn vibrant shades of yellow, orange, and purple in fall shortly after its purple flowers appear. Stiff aster is the only native aster that provides consistent and beautiful fall foliage, and if you have a sunny, dry site you would be remiss not to include this plant. Combine stiff aster with butterfly milkweed (*Asclepias tuberosa*) and little bluestem (*Schizachyrium scoparium*) for a long season of interest. Sun, average to dry soils, zones 3–8.

The wood asters are ideal for dry, shady sites and provide great color and interest in the late summer to early fall garden. Blue wood, or heart-leaved aster (*S. cordifolium*), is the taller of the two, but it is less rambunctious than white wood aster. Blue wood aster grows well in partial sun to dense shade and shows prolific violet flowers for several weeks from late summer through fall. It works very well in combination with wreath goldenrod. Part sun to part shade, average to dry soils, zones 3–8.

White wood aster (*Eurybia divaricata*) is a perfect plant for dense shade and dry, acidic soils. Like blue wood aster, white wood aster blooms heavily in late summer through fall, and seeds itself around with ease to the harshest spots it can find in the garden. White wood aster is a great choice for areas outside the formal, and when not in bloom, it has a nice blue-green leaf. Part sun to part shade, average to dry soils, zones 3–8.

Rue anemone, *Thalictrum thalictroides*

Previously known as *Anemonella*, rue anemone (*Thalictrum thalictroides*) is a diminutive, semi-ephemeral plant that should find a place in every woodland garden in New England. One of the first species to emerge

Rue anemone works well in an early spring container garden.

in spring, rue anemone has foliage that comes up in varying shades of red and purple before eventually turning green. Some plants green up quickly, while others hold tinges of color until late spring and beyond. Flowers are produced soon after the leaves emerge and range from pure white to pink to purple. It's not hard to find double-flowering, sterile forms on the market, but what we love most about growing natural species is that within a few years of planting rue anemone, you will find new seedlings everywhere, and with those new seedlings comes a variety of color shades and forms. Most new plants will be single-flowered and white, but pinks, purples, and some semi-doubles will appear as your patch matures.

We describe rue anemone as semi-ephemeral because most of the plants will follow a typical ephemeral life cycle—emerging early, blooming quickly, and disappearing with the summer heat. However, others will hold their foliage through the summer and sporadically rebloom (albeit lightly) later in the season.

Though not fast growing, rue anemone will fill in the holes in a garden over time, and one of the best garden uses for it is as a fine detail planting along trail edges and in between rocks or larger clumping plants in the garden. Rue anemone will tolerate full sun in spring, but will go dormant more quickly if not shaded by deciduous trees. Between the foliage effect and the long bloom time, rue anemone is an incredibly showy native plant. Part shade to shade, average to moist soils, zones 4–9.

Foamflower, *Tiarella cordifolia* var. *cordifolia*

Foamflower could possibly be the ideal groundcover for the shady garden. It's easy to grow, stunningly beautiful in multiple seasons, and a perfect plant to use as a living mulch. There are two distinct, naturally occurring botanical varieties, one of which clumps while the other spreads. Both are available in the trade, although the clumping form is found far more often than the running form.

The clumping foamflower (*Tiarella cordifolia* var. *collina*) is not native to the New England ecoregions, occurring naturally south of our region. Most of the foamflower cultivars in the trade are selections of this variety, rather than our native *T. cordifolia* var. *cordifolia*, or running foamflower. A true running form, the native variety sends out stolons (aboveground runners, like those of strawberry) and easily spreads throughout the garden, forming a mat of evergreen foliage. When used as a living mulch, often in combination with other shade-loving groundcovers such as wild blue phlox (*Phlox divaricata*) or barren strawberry (*Geum fragarioides*), the native running foamflower is a much more versatile plant than the southern, clumping variety. At Garden in the Woods, we plant foamflower in drifts around taller woodland plants and allow it to fill in all the bare spots in between. The clumping variety simply doesn't work in this manner.

Beautiful white (tinged pink) flowers appear in spring, at the height of peak spring display in New England and overlapping with the flowering time for many of our spring ephemeral species. The flowers last for a few weeks, eventually giving way to small fruits that provide a less substantial, but similar in terms of texture, show immediately after flowering. After flowering and fruiting, foamflower foliage puts on a show of its own. When grown from seed, this plant reveals what makes it so popular in plant breeding programs—each individual plant exhibits a slightly different leaf from its neighbor. Some plants have deep lobes and dark, maroon mottling, while others are entire (not lobed) and highly glossy. In mass plantings, foamflower provides a long season of interest, from early spring flowers to decent fall color and evergreen foliage.

When not in bloom, foamflower leaves provide great texture in a woodland garden.

In the wild, these plants are mainly restricted to moist, rich sites, and though they prefer these conditions, foamflower can be quite drought tolerant once established. With its ability to grow in shade, take the place of mulch, and look great almost all year, foamflower might just be the perfect groundcover for a shady garden. Sun to shade, average soils, zones 3–9.

Fallen Leaves and Groundcovers as Mulch

Mulch plays a useful role in the garden as a temporary soil cover to help prevent erosion, keep weeds down, and retain soil moisture. Rather than buying mulch, we recommend using natural, organic materials that you can recycle from the garden (or from other people's gardens), like fallen leaves, to fill this important need. The beauty of fallen leaves is threefold: They are a natural and abundant resource that almost every gardener has access to; they break down and contribute organic matter to soil, adding fertility and enhancing its ability to retain moisture; and best of all, except for a little labor to collect and spread them, they are free! For all the virtues of fallen leaves as mulch, every gardener's goal should be to not see any mulch beyond spring. For a truly low-maintenance garden, choose plants that act as a living mulch. Mat-forming, low-growing perennials and shrubs like barren strawberry (*Geum fragarioides*) and three-toothed cinquefoil (*Sibbaldiopsis tridentata*) provide all the same functions of bark mulch or leaf litter, but don't need to be reapplied every year.

Bellwort, *Uvularia grandiflora* and *Uvularia sessilifolia*

There are three *Uvularia* in New England, two of which we'll cover here. Although the two species appear quite similar in pictures, they are easily distinguished by their growth habit. Large-flowered bellwort (*Uvularia grandiflora*) is an indispensable New England garden plant. Its graceful, arching stems top out at eighteen inches tall and curl over in classic shepherd's crook form. Each stem terminates in a pale to bright yellow flower, comprised of multiple petals that twist independently. Something about the twist to the petals really lends a sense of whimsy to the garden. The yellow flowers are set off nicely against blues and reds, making bellwort well suited to combinations featuring Virginia bluebells (*Mertensia virginica*) and red trillium (*Trillium erectum*), both of which bloom at the same time. Large-flowered bellwort is tightly clumping, in a manner similar to King Solomon's seal (*Polygonatum biflorum*), and it looks great when popping up out of a shorter groundcover. Part shade to shade, average to moist soils, zones 3–8.

Spreading bellwort (*U. sessilifolia*) has very similar leaves and flowers to its cousin, but its form is distinctly different, allowing it to play a completely different role in the woodland garden. Spreading bellwort grows only to about twelve inches tall (often less), and instead of forming tight clumps it forms loose, spreading patches. With good sun and rich soils, spreading bellwort can form a dense patch, but perhaps it's best used as a loosely spreading groundcover, interplanted with spring ephemerals and other lower-growing perennials like Canada mayflower (*Maianthemum canadense*) or foamflower (*Tiarella cordifolia* var. *cordifolia*). For those who are interested in variegated leaves, there are several cultivars available that offer delicate (not gaudy) variegation, although the natural species is plenty attractive without the additional foliage character. Part shade to shade, average to moist soils, zones 3–8.

Large-flowered bellwort

Blue vervain, *Verbena hastata*

Blue vervain (*Verbena hastata*) is well-known by herbalists but less commonly used by ornamental gardeners. Though the flowers are quite small, they pack a punch of color and are arranged in such a way as to still put on quite a show. The flowers are a rich hue of purple that flirts with true blue at times. Small tubular flowers are arranged in multiple pyramids that are further arranged into a larger pyramid. (Pyramid power enthusiasts, this is the plant for you!)

The open and delicate nature of this species contrasts wonderfully with stiff or broad textures, and it looks just as good next to grasses and irises as it does next to ferns or rose milkweed (*Asclepias incarnata*). In fact, a combination of blue vervain, blue flag iris (*Iris versicolor*), and rose milkweed makes a perfect trio to ring pond or creek edges or any moist meadow.

Small iridescent sweat bees can be found visiting the flowers, and the leaves act as host sites for a handful of different caterpillars. In the wild, this plant is found in moist meadows and wetland edges, and in the garden it's best to avoid planting it in overly dry sites. Sun to part sun, moist to wet soils, zones 3–9.

Blue vervain

New York ironweed looks great poking up through winterberry in any moist area of the garden.

New York ironweed, *Vernonia noveboracensis*

New York ironweed (*Vernonia noveboracensis*) is not for the faint of heart. It is a robust plant with deep, rich purple flowers that often towers above other plants. It's found on lakesides or in moist meadows, among Joe-Pye weed, rose milkweed, and blue vervain, where it normally stretches at least a foot above all its neighbors.

New York ironweed's flowers appear in midsummer and tend to coincide with a variety of other native plants that grow in similar conditions. They are royal purple in color, and each cluster is an arrangement of several flowers comprised of narrow, purple petals that radiate from the central eye and branch on the ends. The resulting look is a combination of order and chaos and is interesting not only for its color but for its structure as well.

This plant works particularly well in combination with broad-leaved mountain mint (*Pycnanthemum muticum*) and any of the dozens of tall yellow flowering perennials native to New England. The size of New York ironweed means it works wonderfully as a tall accent growing among smaller plants that do well in similar site conditions. Conversely, New York ironweed is an ideal candidate for perennial pruning in early summer to keep it a little shorter in stature. Wait until just after its initial spring growth spurt before cutting the plant back heavily in June. The result will be a plant that tops out at around three to four feet rather than the typical six to eight feet.

New York ironweed's fruits are not nearly as showy as the flowers, but still provide nice textural interest in the garden that coincidentally contrasts nicely with the fruits of many of those tall yellow perennials mentioned earlier. Sun to part sun, average to wet soils, zones 3–9.

Culver's root, *Veronicastrum virginicum*

Culver's root (*Veronicastrum virginicum*) lends wonderful architecture to the garden. While it has attractive flowers, its structure and form are reason enough to find a spot for this plant in the garden. Culver's root is comprised of many narrow, upright vertical stems, making it well suited as an architectural accent at the back of a perennial border. Running all along the stems are whorls of leaves spaced out at regular intervals that give Culver's root a rigid yet playful appearance. Although some of the traits plant nerds tend to drool over are obscure and visible only to those who really pay attention to such things, the growth form of this plant is really something to behold and can be appreciated by the novice and the seasoned gardener alike.

While the form of Culver's root is enough reason to plant it, the flowers are also quite beautiful. In addition to adding a midsummer burst of white to the garden, the flowers further enhance the plant's vertical structure. The flower color is usually white, but sometimes ranges into light pinks and even purple on occasion. The arrangement of the stems and flowers allows this plant to catch the wind nicely, creating a beautiful waving effect on a breezy day.

Though perfectly fine in average garden soils, Culver's root really shines in moist areas. Equally happy standing alone on a pond edge, when it is interplanted among hundreds of other plants in a moist meadow alongside asters and ironweed, Culver's root's unique form and impressive floral display help it to stand out even when mixed in with other species. Sun to part shade, average to moist soils, zones 3–9.

Culver's root
PHOTO COURTESY OF NEW ENGLAND WILD FLOWER SOCIETY

Bird's foot violet

Bird's foot violet, *Viola pedata*

Violets have an unfortunate reputation as garden weeds, and while some may deserve that reputation, there are more than twenty-five violet species found in New England. To label all of them weeds would be doing a disservice to this important group of plants. There are several violets worth considering for use in the native plant garden, but one that rises above all others for ornamental impact is bird's foot violet (*Viola pedata*).

Though small in stature, bird's foot violet packs a visual punch of both color and texture. Violets are notoriously difficult to tell apart when not in bloom because so many of them have such similar leaves. That's not true of this species. The plant is well named for its deeply lobed leaves that resemble a bird's feet. The structure of the leaves as well as their tendency to catch and hold droplets of water makes this plant visually interesting whether in bloom or not. Light to bright blue-purple flowers appear in early spring and bloom through early summer, sometimes producing a second smaller flush of flowers in fall. Each flower is roughly one-third as large as the plant is tall, making the flowers appear almost massive relative to the plant overall.

Tolerant of dry sites and some shade, bird's foot violet is easy to find in the garden. They are small enough to dot in among larger perennials and look great planted under shrubs and trees. Once established, new seedlings will start popping up within a few feet of the original plants and will slowly begin filling in any bare areas nearby. Violets are essential as host sites for a large number of caterpillars, including the regal fritillary, a beautiful but uncommon visitor to New England. Sun to part sun, dry soils, zones 3–9.

Trees and Shrubs

Like herbaceous perennials, trees and shrubs are perennial plants, persisting for longer than one season. The plants in this chapter all have aboveground parts that are "lignified," or woody, and so can be used to add structure to the garden. In New England especially, where long winters leave many of us yearning for warmer temperatures, trees and shrubs add interest to the winter garden with features like evergreen foliage, colorful or otherwise interesting bare stems, or persistent fruit that remains showy long past fall. Unlike herbaceous perennials, the woody stems of trees and shrubs are a semipermanent fixture in the garden, and the mature height and width of these plants should be understood and accounted for when siting them in the garden. Avoid the mistake of planting an oak tree under a power line, for example, or using a large evergreen shrub like great rosebay as a foundation plant under a window. Most of the plants in this chapter have multiple seasons of interest—from early spring flowers to great fall color—and all of them offer habitat or forage for local wildlife.

Maple, *Acer* spp.

It's hard to walk too far in New England without bumping into a maple tree. Of the four species covered here, the most recognizable of them, the sugar maple (*Acer saccharum*), is ubiquitous throughout much of New England, particularly in the colder northern states. The effects of climate change and introduced insect pests like Asian longhorned beetle may ultimately spell the demise of this important cultural icon, which provides an outstanding display for leaf peepers in fall. But for now, we can still enjoy its fall color, ranging from yellow to red and every color in between. Sugar maple is happiest in dry soils with good drainage, and is the primary source of sap for the maple syrup industry. In addition to its incredible fall foliage, sugar maple has very distinctive, platy bark ranging from gray to light brown in color. Given room to spread its canopy, sugar maple is an impressive and long-lived tree. Sun to part shade, dry to average soils, zones 3–8.

In contrast to sugar maple, red maple (*A. rubrum*) is happiest in wet soils, where its vibrant red flowers appear in early spring before its leaves. Interestingly, red maple is polygamodioecious, a very technical way of saying that some trees only produce male flowers, some only produce female flowers, and some produce both male and female flowers. Like sugar maple, red maple has impressive fall color, normally red, though occasionally yellow to orange. Despite its other common name, swamp maple, *A. rubrum* is a fairly adaptable species that can grow anywhere from standing water to fairly dry sites. Sun to part shade, wet to dry soils, zones 3–9.

Silver maple (*A. saccharinum*) has perhaps the most interesting foliage of all the native maples, featuring deep sinuses and a light-colored underside to the leaf that appears to shimmer in the slightest breeze. Often thought of as a messy tree, silver maple tends to frequently drop small branches, especially when planted on a dry site. A fast-growing tree found naturally along streambanks, silver maple's fall display is yellow in color but can't compare with the vibrant hues of red and sugar maple. Sun to part shade, average to moist soils, zones 3–9.

Striped maple bark provides tremendous winter interest.

The smallest of the lot, striped maple (*A. pensylvanicum*) is a fantastic medium-size tree for an ornamental garden, thanks in part to its unique bark. Especially pronounced on young stems, striped maple bark is usually a light green (sometimes darker), broken up by vertical white and black stripes, making it especially appealing in winter. Part sun to part shade, average to moist soils, zones 3–7.

The leaves of striped maple are much larger than those of red maple.

Serviceberry, *Amelanchier* spp.

The many species of serviceberry (*Amelanchier* spp.), also known as sugar plum, shadbush, shadblow, Juneberry, saskatoon, and about a half dozen other names, can be large shrubs to small multistemmed trees. Similar in stature, serviceberry can replace crabapples, ornamental pears, or Asian cherries in a native plant garden. Abundant white flowers coat the branches in spring, giving rise to red berries that mature to purple when ripe. Birds usually get to the berries well before they ripen, but if you can beat them to the punch, we highly recommend serviceberry as a tasty treat. The flavor is a combination of a sweet blueberry and a tart cherry. When cooked into pies, they are often referred to as sugarplums. Serviceberry is often grown for its vibrant fall foliage, which ranges from red to orange. Most of the cultivars on the market (of which there are many) have been selected for their growth form and fall color.

Throughout much of New England, winter moth, an introduced Eurasian insect pest, strips serviceberry of its foliage in spring. Although plants usually rebound with a second flush of leaves, repeated attacks year after year may eventually kill an otherwise healthy plant. Fortunately, University of Massachusetts entomologists have been working with a biological control that shows promise for controlling winter moth across the region. A host-specific insect called a tachinid fly lays its eggs on the buds of plants that winter moth caterpillars eat, where unknowing caterpillars ingest them. Several weeks later, when the caterpillars pupate and fall to the ground, the fly larvae parasitize and kill them. While successful control across the entire region may be years away, winter moth has been successfully controlled in Wellesley, Massachusetts, thanks to the introduction of this biological control.

Smooth serviceberry (*A. laevis*) is the best choice for a tree form or large clumping form, usually growing to a mature size of fifteen to twenty-five feet. Sun to part shade, dry to moist soils, zones 3–8.

Eastern shadbush (*A. canadensis*) is a true shrub form, with many stems usually growing to about the eight- to fifteen-foot range. Sun to part shade, dry to average soils, zones 4–9.

The vast majority of the cultivars on the market are various forms of *A. grandiflora*, a natural hybrid between downy shadbush (*A. arborea*) and smooth serviceberry. While each cultivar has some unique attribute, most of them are multistemmed shrubs that grow in the fifteen- to twenty-five-foot range. Part shade to shade, average to moist soils, zones 4–8.

Serviceberry

Bearberry, *Arctostaphylos uva-ursi*

Most plants, native or not, have particular seasons of interest, and while many shine at a single time of year, it's often difficult to find a species with multiple seasons of interest. So when we stumble across a plant that looks good year-round (yes, including winter), it tends to join the top of our lists of favorite plants. *Arctostaphylos uva-ursi* literally translates to "berry of the bear," hence the common name bearberry. This plant flowers in spring, fruits in summer, turns brilliant shades of purple-red in fall, and is evergreen to boot—four full seasons of interest!

Like many other members of the heath family, this species produces bell-shaped flowers that are a favorite of bees. The flowers range from pure white to pink and contrast wonderfully with the deep green, glossy leaves. By summer the flowers have passed, but they are followed by large, vibrant red berries about the size of cranberries. A good winter forage for birds, the berries are unfortunately not edible for humans.

Bearberry has bright red fruits and glossy evergreen foliage.

Bearberry's winter foliage ranges from bright red to burgundy.
CAYTE McDONOUGH

They aren't poisonous either, so have no fear planting bearberry where young children might be attracted to it.

In fall, the deep green foliage begins to turn various shades of purple and red, a color it retains all winter. In coastal sites in the wild, bearberry often forms vast colonies on sandy banks in full sun. A single plant can grow to an impressive width, forming an incredibly dense ground-cover. Bearberry does not grow taller than a few inches and in winter is obscured by snow cover in New England. As a coastal species, bearberry is salt-, wind-, and drought-tolerant, making it an almost ideal parking lot plant. Plant it along a driveway or a sidewalk that gets treated with salt in the winter and it will not skip a beat. Its only strict cultural requirement appears to be good drainage and a decent amount of sun. This is not a plant that can withstand any standing water. Sun, average to dry, well-drained soils, zones 1–8.

Chokeberry, *Aronia* spp.

The chokeberries (*Aronia* spp.) have been cursed with an unfortunate common name. But gardeners would be wise to overlook this travesty and take a second look at this attractive group of native shrubs. In the wild, chokeberries grow as sprawling shrubs on semishady wetland edges. In the garden, they are gorgeous, multistemmed shrubs that become very drought tolerant once established. Pure white flower petals are offset by red stamens in spring, followed by either red or black berries that are high in antioxidants. In fact, despite their common name, chokeberries are a trendy superfood, perfectly edible, albeit quite bitter (hence the name "chokeberry"). While the berries are still present, the foliage turns deep maroon to bright red, putting on an impressive display.

Red chokeberry (*A. arbutifolia*) is arguably the showier of the two native New England species, featuring bright red berries that really pop against deep green leaves. Because the color of the berry is so close to the eventual color of its fall foliage, red chokeberry fruit tends to hide in plain sight once its leaves color up. In contrast, the black berries of black chokeberry (*A. melanocarpa*) become more visible as its foliage turns color. Black chokeberry is considered the tastier of the two species, with the bitter taste of the berries being (slightly) offset by an inherent sweetness.

From full sun to part shade, moist to dry sites, chokeberry can play an important role in the edible garden, the bird garden, the butterfly garden, or just about anywhere in the garden that could use a little more pop in fall. Sun to part shade, dry to moist soils, zones 4–9 (3–9 for *A. melanocarpa*).

Red chokeberry

Pawpaw, *Asimina triloba*

Pawpaw (*Asimina triloba*) has received a lot of attention lately as the interest in edible landscapes has grown. Though much more common farther south, this species is nonetheless native to New England's ecoregions, where it can be found in rich forests and floodplains. In cultivation, it is tolerant of average soils, but the richer the soils, the better the crop of pawpaws you will receive. The fruits are the largest edible fruits native to the United States, and if not for their inability to store well, we

The fruits of pawpaw are delectable.
PHOTO COURTESY OF NATIVESCAPESMA

would likely find them in every grocery store in the United States. The flavor is phenomenal, tasting something like a combination of mango, pear, and banana and with a texture reminiscent of custard. If you find yourself with an abundance of them, they can easily be converted into preserves or baked into pies, custards, or flan, but fresh fruits are good for a week at the most before they start to soften and the flavor dissipates.

As a landscape tree, they produce mesmerizing but small, deep maroon flowers that open about the same time as the tree's leaves unfurl and are easy to miss if you're not looking for them. The leaves are large and unlobed and look as if they would fit into a tropical jungle as easily as the New England landscape. New leaves emerge with a wonderful gloss that holds for quite a while, only dissipating as more new leaves emerge. Even late in the season, the youngest leaves still hold a shine that makes them very ornamental.

Especially in moist sites, pawpaw forms colonies with multiple stems emerging around a large main stem. Left untrimmed, they form a dense jungle-like tangle, but when thinned, they let in enough light for an underplanting of other edibles such as ramps (*Allium tricoccum*) or fiddlehead ferns (*Matteuccia struthiopteris*). They can also be grown as a single-stemmed specimen with minimal effort. Sun to part shade, average to moist soils, zones 4–9.

Birch, *Betula* spp.

There are nine native birch species in New England, ranging from fast-growing pioneer species like gray birch (*Betula populifolia*) to slower-growing, long-lived species like yellow birch (*B. alleghaniensis*). Regardless of the species, birches are easily among the top ten woody plants in terms of value for wildlife. Birches are major host trees for dozens if not hundreds of butterfly and moth species and important habitat for nesting birds.

B. papyrifera goes by several common names, including paper birch, white birch, and canoe birch, and is likely the most recognizable species. Its characteristic white exfoliating bark is probably what most people have in mind when they think about birches. In the wild, paper birch trees are early colonizers after disturbance, like logging or fire, and they normally succumb to the competition of later successional and longer-lived tree species, which eventually outgrow them and shade them out. In the garden, paper birch can be an attractive specimen but, especially in southern New England, it should still be viewed as a fairly short-lived plant. Part shade to sun, average to moist soils, zones 2–6.

Gray birch (*B. populifolia*) is similar to paper birch, but not as attractive and slightly smaller at maturity. The trunk is covered in mildly exfoliating white bark that, unfortunately, cannot hold a candle to paper birch. Its leaves have a long tapering point that lends some interest. Gray birch is more heat tolerant and is a better choice if looking for a white-barked specimen in southern New England. Bronze birch borer attacks both species, especially when the trees are heat stressed. Sun to part shade, dry to moist soils, zones 3–7.

River birch (*B. nigra*) is the most widely used of all native birch species. It seems that 99 percent of the plants on the landscape are a single cultivar called 'Heritage,' a selection with showier bark that it retains well into maturity. In the case of river birch, *B. nigra* 'Heritage' is thought to be much more ornamental than the natural species, and therefore has been propagated and distributed across the globe. All 'Heritage' plants are genetically identical, resulting from cuttings off a single plant. These clonal plants are of particular concern when one considers the relative

Yellow birch is one of several species of birch native to New England.

susceptibility of river birch on the landscape to new pests and diseases. With genetic diversity comes greater ability for a population of plants to resist damage from new pests and diseases, or from changes in climate. Consider this when choosing to plant river birch in your garden and look for the natural species rather than this popular cultivar.

Whether 'Heritage' or the natural species, river birch is a beautiful tree with white- to salmon-colored bark that peels in a manner similar to paper birch. River birch is a medium-size tree, growing to about forty feet tall, and is much longer lived than paper or gray birch. Sun to part shade, average to moist soils, zones 4–9.

Yellow birch is underappreciated in the ornamental landscape, but is a striking tree that should be used more often. Slower growing and longer lived than all previously mentioned species, yellow birch will eventually reach up to sixty feet in height. The golden yellow bark is striking as it exfoliates, and fall color is a brilliant but fleeting yellow. Yellow birch, owing to its sweetness and characteristic flavor, is the species used in making birch beer. In fact, you can make a very tasty tea by adding young twigs to simmering water. Neither yellow birch nor river birch is bothered by bronze birch borer. Sun to shade, average to moist soils, zones 3–7.

Musclewood, *Carpinus caroliniana*

Musclewood (*Carpinus caroliniana*) is a good example of a native plant that is often overlooked because of its more popular cousin, in this case

Musclewood

European hornbeam (*C. betulus*). Both plants are similar in appearance, with a trunk that resembles a tense, muscular arm. But where the European hornbeam is long lived and formal in appearance, our native musclewood is a shorter-lived, smaller understory tree with a far less formal appearance.

Despite its less formal appearance, musclewood has some amazing attributes that make it a unique and interesting choice for the garden. Its smooth, light-gray bark glistens after a rain, further accentuating the sculptural appearance of its trunk and branches. It has a graceful, arching branching habit that can nicely frame a walking path through the garden when these trees are planted on either side.

Another common name for this tree is blue beech, referring to its slightly blue-green foliage that is similar in appearance to the leaves of our native beech (*Fagus sylvatica*).

Musclewood naturally grows in floodplains, but is happy in a range of soil moisture levels. Like many small understory trees, musclewood can grow in fairly deep shade, where it will have sparse foliage and appear more sculptural. It also does quite well in sun, where it will appear fuller and where more of the interesting bark will be obscured by its attractive foliage. Part sun to shade, average to moist soils, zones 3–8.

Shagbark hickory, *Carya ovata*

Shagbark hickory (*Carya ovata*) is another great tree for ecological value and is host to the hickory horned devil, the largest North American caterpillar, which eventually becomes the regal moth, the largest moth north of Mexico. In addition to its value ecologically, shagbark hickory is an elegant tree, with a distinctive narrow, upright form that lends outstanding vertical structure to the landscape. Though the bark doesn't "shag" when young, mature hickories have some of the coolest bark of any native tree. Large sections of its outer bark peel off the main trunk in vertical strips, giving the tree its very fitting name, shagbark. The leaves are compound, lending a soft texture to its otherwise rigid form, and the fall color is a brilliant yellow that looks backlit.

Edible plant enthusiasts seek out shagbark hickory for its nuts, which happen to be incredibly tasty. They are excellent raw and even better when roasted. The nuts can also make a tasty drink, which may be the origin of the common name, hickory. Native Americans introduced early settlers to a drink made of young hickory nuts mashed into a paste and mixed with water to the consistency of a milkshake. This drink (which was apparently loved by children far and wide) was known as "powcohiccora," but because settlers had trouble pronouncing the name, they shortened it to hickory. Sun to part shade, dry to moist soils, zones 4–9.

The aptly named shagbark hickory

Redbud

Redbud, *Cercis canadensis*

Redbud (*Cercis canadensis*) has perhaps the showiest flowers of any native tree in New England. A very loud fuchsia explodes from the branches of this plant in mid-spring before its leaves emerge. With an arching habit and heart-shaped leaves, redbud is a very attractive small flowering tree that should easily find a home in any New England garden.

Perhaps best known for its impressive floral display, redbud exhibits a trait called "cauliflory," a term that simply means "stem flower" and refers to its ability to flower directly out of its trunk and large branches. Where most flowering trees have blossoms only on young twigs and stems, it's not unusual to see clusters of four to six small, fuchsia flowers poking out of the main trunk of a mature redbud tree, adding to its intrigue.

Redbud is a member of the pea family, with characteristic peapods following its flowers. It produces a lot of fruit, making it a frequent "volunteer" in other parts of the garden. As a member of the pea family, redbud is able to absorb atmospheric nitrogen from the air and as a result can grow in nutrient-poor soils.

Redbud's leaves are heart shaped and quite attractive. Several cultivars are available in the trade, including several with purple foliage. A natural botanical variety, *C. canadensis* var. *alba*, has white flowers and is also easy to find for sale. Sun to part shade, dry to moist soils, zones 4–9.

Redbud blooms profusely in spring.

Atlantic white cedar, *Chamaecyparis thyoides*

Scale-leaved evergreen plants are difficult to come by in New England. A few notable exceptions are Atlantic white cedar (*Chamaecyparis thyoides*), arborvitae (*Thuja occidentalis*), and eastern red cedar (*Juniperus virginiana*). Atlantic white cedar is a great choice for an evergreen tree or large shrub for moist to wet soils. At first glance, it appears quite similar to arborvitae, a much more common landscape plant, but there are several distinct differences that make this perhaps a more attractive ornamental plant.

As a functional landscape element, Atlantic white cedar works quite well as a living fence, dividing garden rooms, providing wind screening, or serving as a visual barrier to neighboring properties. But, owing to its attractive blue-green foliage, Atlantic white cedar also works well as a specimen tree, providing winter interest and a vertical element in the garden. In addition to its attractive foliage, Atlantic white cedar's bark can be quite beautiful, as it acquires a reddish tinge with age that contrasts nicely with the blue-green foliage.

Though not quite at the same level as balsam fir (*Abies balsamea*), the foliage of Atlantic white cedar has a spicy freshness when crushed, and is best enjoyed by brushing up against trailside plants on a warm sunny day. Sun to part sun, moist to wet soils, zones 4–9.

Atlantic white cedar

White fringetree

White fringetree, *Chionanthus virginicus*

White fringetree (*Chionanthus virginicus*) is one of those plants that people seem to admire, but it is often overlooked or forgotten about, despite an impressive floral display in late spring. We suppose this can be forgiven, as it is fairly nondescript when not in bloom, but it flowers at the perfect time, during a lull in New England gardens. Blooming at about the same time its foliage emerges in mid- to late spring, white fringetree flowers offer a wonderfully sweet fragrance, something like a cup of tea with a whole lot of honey. Aside from the fragrance, the flowers are interesting—while not necessarily attractive individually, in masses, the flowers of this plant make an impressive, airy, and open display.

White fringetree can be used as either a single-stemmed, small flowering tree or as a large, multistemmed shrub, similar in form to witch hazel (*Hamamelis virginiana*). It has an irregular, open vase shape as a shrub, with several stems emerging from the base. As a member of the ash (or olive) family, white fringetree is susceptible to the introduced insect pest, emerald ash borer. While this insect has not widely invaded New England, it has been spotted in Connecticut, Massachusetts, and New Hampshire. This is not reason enough to avoid white fringetree at this point, but it is something to keep in mind if you are considering adding this plant, or any plant in the Oleaceae family to your garden. Part shade to sun, moist to dry soils, zones 4–9.

Summersweet, *Clethra alnifolia*

With all the talk about plants for pollinators and wildlife value, we sometimes forget that gardens are meant for human enjoyment as much as anything. One of the best attributes plants provide for our enjoyment in a garden is fragrance, and summersweet (*Clethra alnifolia*) is easily one of the nicest-smelling plants on the planet. The fact that it's also a pollinator magnet makes it an outstanding plant for both people and pollinators. The scent is wonderfully sweet, but with a touch of spice that adds depth to the fragrance.

Along wetland edges or lakesides, summersweet often forms dense colonies, but in gardens it rarely suckers, instead creating a tight clump of multiple narrow, wandering stems, each covered in white (rarely tinged pink) flowers in midsummer. The fragrance is not the only redeeming quality of these blooms, as they are incredibly showy and often covered in native bees.

Though happy in moist sites, summersweet is perfectly capable of growing in average garden soils and will tolerate drier conditions once established. Fall color is a rich yellow and looks great combined with the bright red berries of winterberry (*Ilex verticillata*), which can often be found growing in similar conditions. Throw in a spicebush (*Lindera benzoin*) and you've got spring, summer, fall, and early winter interest all covered. Sun to part sun, average to wet soils, zones 4–9.

Summersweet

Sweetfern

Sweetfern, *Comptonia peregrina*

Sweet fern (*Comptonia peregrina*) is a shrub masquerading as a fern. The foliage both looks like a fern and smells wonderfully sweet when ruffled, lending the plant its common name. The scent is reminiscent of Cinnamon Toast Crunch cereal, and whenever possible we like to plant sweetfern along trailsides where visitors brush up against the foliage as they stroll through the garden.

Sweetfern does just as well in full sun as it does in partial shade and is tolerant of extremely dry soils. Full sun and dry soils seems to accentuate the scent, so keep this in mind when trying to find the right spot for one in the garden.

This species doesn't look bad as a specimen, but it really shines when planted in masses. It can be used as an effective taller groundcover to frame larger shrubs or trees, and can look especially nice when planted around large boulders.

Sweetfern is often touted as an edible species, and though it doesn't make a half bad tea, we've never found the fruits to be particularly tasty. It does, however, make a great potpourri. Sun, dry soils, zones 2–6.

Hazelnut, *Corylus americana*

Hazelnut (*Corylus americana*) is woefully underused in the ornamental garden. Edible enthusiasts know this plant well, but it is rarely planted for its beauty, which starts with very early spring flowers and finishes with incredible fall color. Fall foliage ranges from yellow to red to purple and is on par with other native shrubs celebrated for their foliage displays like highbush blueberry (*Vaccinium corymbosum*) and witherod (*Viburnum nudum* var. *cassinoides*).

The nuts themselves really are amazingly tasty, though if grown on the edge of a woodland they are usually snatched up by squirrels before people can get to them. When grown in open fields, where raptors fly above, people have a much better chance of getting a meal's worth. Though happy to grow on woodland edges, hazelnuts are also amazingly tolerant plants: full sun, blasting winds, salt spray, dry soils—no problem.

We watch for the flowers each spring. They are beautiful in their own way but are also so small that you'd hardly notice them unless you were looking for them. The reason we watch for them is because we think of them as harbingers of spring. When the skunk cabbage (*Symplocarpus foetidus*) begins blooming, you know spring is close; when the hazelnuts bloom, spring is here. Sun to part shade, dry to average soils, zones 4–8.

Hazelnut's fall color is spectacular.

The female flowers of hazelnut are tiny but beautiful.

Wintergreen, *Gaultheria procumbens*

One of a short list of plants native to northern acid forests, wintergreen (*Gaultheria procumbens*) can be found just about anywhere where conifers make up a part of the canopy. Dark, glossy, evergreen leaves hold their color until fall, when they turn varying degrees of red and maroon depending on the amount of sun they receive. In dark places they often simply darken to a deeper green before lightening up again in the spring. Wintergreen flowers are similar to those of blueberries, and the bright white stands out strongly against the dark green leaves.

Bright red fruits follow spring flowers, and both the fruits and leaves have a characteristic wintergreen flavor. The leaves are great as a trail nibble or for tea, and throwing a handful of fruits into a fruit salad adds a very unique touch of flavor.

Though tolerant of dry sites in the wild, wintergreen is easier to establish in moist soils in the garden. Acid soils are essential; plant wintergreen among blueberries and bunchberries and you'll have your own little ode to Maine in your garden. Part shade to shade, average soils, zones 3–8.

Wintergreen

Witch hazel, *Hamamelis virginiana*

New England's latest blooming shrub may very well be sitting in your medicine cabinet as you read this book. Witch hazel (*Hamamelis virginiana*) is better known as a skin tonic than as a landscape shrub, and that is something we'd like to see changed. This species has a lot to offer the native plant gardener, and yet we find they are rarely used in built landscapes. Though exclusively found in moist to wet areas in the wild, witch hazel is quite drought tolerant once established in the garden, and will grow in full sun to fairly deep shade.

Beautiful spider-like yellow flowers bloom in late fall, often opening before foliage turns a vibrant yellow. The contrast of bright yellow flowers against rich green foliage is striking, and the fact that the flowers become invisible after fall color sets in can be forgiven in light of the brilliant foliage display.

The foliage has wonderful wavy edges (technically called crenate), and the form of the overall shrub is vase-shaped with wandering branches that look excellent when silhouetted against the sun or with a light covering of snow. Interplant witch hazel with winterberry (*Ilex verticillata*) for a great combination of yellow flowers/foliage and red berries. Part sun to part shade, average to wet soils, zones 3–8.

Witch hazel

The fertile flowers of smooth hydrangea offer a pollen and nectar reward that double-flowered cultivars like 'Annabelle' lack.

Smooth hydrangea, *Hydrangea arborescens*

Smooth hydrangea (*Hydrangea arborescens*) is rarely sold as anything but the cultivar, 'Annabelle.' Although 'Annabelle' is a great plant, the natural species produces a more delicate lacecap flower that is more subtle and less boastful than the cultivar. With larger, outer, sterile petals that act to attract the pollinators into the smaller, inner, fertile petals, the natural species also provides more support for pollinators than the entirely sterile flowers of 'Annabelle.' A lack of fertile flowers and the nectar and pollen they produce does not mean that 'Annabelle' offers no value for wildlife, as its leaves still act as effective host sites for caterpillars—but it does reduce its value overall. We like to plant both 'Annabelle' and the natural species so that we provide the show of 'Annabelle' and the ecological value of the natural flowers.

Though happy in sunny, moist environments, smooth hydrangea is also perfectly happy growing in drier, partially shaded sites where it can form a loose colony. In addition to its adaptability, it can be cut back hard each year, making it a good candidate for planting as foundation plants, where falling snow can do damage to other shrubs. Part sun to shade, average soils, zones 4–9.

'Annabelle' hydrangea

Holly, *Ilex spp.*

Hollies (*Ilex* spp.) are an extremely diverse group of plants, including much more than the sharply pointed, evergreen plants with bright red berries that typically come to mind. Most of these "Christmas hollies" are Chinese species, but our native American holly, (*Ilex opaca*) gives us a nice winter show. Unlike the Chinese species, American hollies are more tree than shrub; they are slow growing and a bit gangly in youth but become quite beautiful as they mature. When grown alone in sun or light shade, they mature into narrow pyramids with a glossy evergreen, sharply pointed leaves. In the wild, American holly grows in dense stands, causing individual plants to lose their tight pyramidal form and revealing more of the light, smooth bark. Walking through a grove of American holly is like walking into another world. Birds love them both for their berries and for the protective cover they offer. Keep them protected from strong winter winds, which can dry out the leaves, leading to winter burn. Sun to part shade, average soils, zones 5–9.

Winterberry holly fruits persist well into winter.

The most well-known native holly is likely winterberry holly (*I. verticillata*), which is often the showiest plant in the winter garden. Its vibrant red berries develop in early fall and often persist into winter before birds finally get to them. Be cautious of any cultivars that claim the berries last through the winter. If your goal is to support a healthy ecosystem, the last thing you want is a berry that birds won't eat. Winterberry holly prefers wet soils but grows well when planted in average garden soil that does not get too dry at any point during the year. Like all hollies, winterberry holly is dioecious, meaning there are separate male and female plants. Only the female plants bear fruit, but both male and female plants are necessary for cross pollination to ensure fruit set. Sun to part shade, average to wet soils, zones 3–9.

For those looking for the formal effect of a broad-leaved evergreen shrub that resembles boxwood, inkberry (*Ilex glabra*) is a great choice. Boxwood is not native and despite myriad pests and diseases that inflict them, people still seem to use them in their gardens. Inkberry is an evergreen shrub with small, glossy, deep green leaves that contrast with its small flowers in a way that shows them off better than any other holly. The fruit on female plants is a deep purple to almost black, though they tend to blend in with inkberry's dark foliage. Sun to part sun, dry to wet soils, zones 5–9.

Inkberry has deep green evergreen foliage.

Eastern red cedar, *Juniperus virginiana*

As a garden plant, there are certainly better options than eastern red cedar (*Juniperus virginiana*). But understanding the various attributes of this plant may make a gardener consider finding a spot to let one grow in the ornamental garden. Not a true cedar, eastern red cedar is actually a type of juniper. It has two distinct leaf types: awl-shaped young leaves and more scale-like older leaves. One remarkable thing about eastern red cedar is the variability that exists between plants. In an open meadow that's been fallow and unmowed for several years, it's not uncommon to find eastern red cedars in a range of colors, from blue-green to reddish, in forms ranging from tall and upright to broad-spreading.

An early successional species, eastern red cedar moves into an area quickly after natural disturbance such as fire or a windstorm, or when an old agricultural field has been left fallow. Here, these trees provide important habitat and food for birds like cedar waxwings, which enjoy eating its berry-like blue cones. It is tolerant of nutrient-poor, dry soils and full sun exposure, and helps provide some soil stabilization before dominant forest canopy trees like oaks, hickories, and maples can recolonize an area.

Eastern red cedar has remarkably rot-resistant wood; indeed, the benches at Garden in the Woods are all crafted from local cedar. In addition to its value as a rot-resistant local lumber, eastern red cedar is host to a fascinating fungus called cedar apple rust. Like all rusts, cedar apple rust is a dual-host fungus, spending the winter on eastern red cedar and the summer infecting the leaves of fruit-bearing trees and shrubs in the rose family, like apples and serviceberries. While most gardeners (and apple growers) may not appreciate the unique beauty of this fungus, we think it is a sight to behold in spring. Gelatinous orange spikes burst from a gall that developed on the stem of eastern red cedar the previous fall. I'm always reminded of Sideshow Bob's hair (he's a character from *The Simpsons*) when I happen upon one in spring. Now if that's not enough to convince you to plant an eastern red cedar, I don't know what else we could say. Sun to light shade, average to dry soils, zones 4–9.

Eastern red cedar

Mountain laurel

Mountain laurel, *Kalmia latifolia*

Mountain laurel (*Kalmia latifolia*) has one of the most interesting and exquisite flowers of our entire native flora. The typical flower starts off as a bright pink, star-shaped bud that opens up to a slightly rounded flower, usually of a much lighter pink hue, often with dark pink lines inside. There is a certain amount of variation from one individual to the next; some plants are light pink, others dark pink, others white, and the amount of coloration on the inside of the petals ranges greatly as well. With this amount of natural variation, no wonder there is a glut of cultivars available.

The stems have a wonderful wandering aspect that really shows off well when these shrubs are planted in masses, and the glossy evergreen leaves contrast with the peeling bark to lend an air of ancientness to the shrub. Standing alone, the plants can sometimes look leggy, but when planted in groups or underplanted with an herbaceous layer, any sense of legginess quickly disappears. This is a subtle but exquisite shrub in the winter landscape.

Mountain laurel does not grow well when planted in areas that lack a sandy component, so when planting one in the garden, it's important to choose a well-drained site. When well-sited mountain laurel is a beautiful shrub, especially in the winter garden; if the correct conditions don't exist, pick another plant. Sun to part shade, average to dry soils, zones 5–9.

Spicebush, *Lindera benzoin*

Spicebush (*Lindera benzoin*) is one of those shrubs that everyone seems to fall in love with, and yet it is still relatively unheard of in the larger horticultural trade. In the wild, it grows in moist, shady sites, often near streams or on wetland edges and almost always is found growing alongside witch hazel (*Hamamelis virginiana*). In cultivation, spicebush is perfectly suited to average garden soils as long as it is not growing in full sun.

The small yellow flowers of spicebush appear in early spring ahead of the leaves, and despite their small size, they are very visible on otherwise bare branches. A while after the flowers have passed, bright red berries appear on female plants (like holly, spicebush also is dioecious), much to the delight of veeries, wood thrushes, and catbirds.

Spicebush berries are edible to people but produce such a punch of flavor that they are used more as seasoning than as fresh eating. The flavor is somewhere between allspice and juniper. In addition to the

Spicebush in fall

berries, the stems make a wonderful tea that is said to be magical for fighting off the common cold and is packed with vitamin C.

The leaves are host sites for the spicebush swallowtail, which hosts only on spicebush and sassafras (*Sassafras albidum*). Look for rolled leaves in mid- to late season and you'll find these adorable caterpillars rolled up inside. In fall the leaves turn a nice rich yellow, which really acts to brighten up an otherwise dark woodland scene wonderfully. Part shade to shade, average to moist soils, zones 4–9.

Spicebush swallowtail may be the most adorable caterpillar in New England.

Sweetgum, *Liquidambar styraciflua*

One of the landscape characteristics that make New England unique is its abundant forests, which burst with color in fall. For leaf-peeping tourists and garden enthusiasts, sugar maple (*Acer saccharum*) is perhaps the most recognized fall beauty, but the less common sweetgum (*Liquidambar styraciflua*) has equally brilliant fall color. The foliage is distinctly star-shaped and often quite glossy. The unique shape and texture of the foliage causes visitors to Garden in the Woods to do a double take when they happen upon a specimen planted near our Lily Pond.

Sweetgum has a stately habit, upright and oval, becoming more open with maturity. A large century-old specimen at the Brooklyn Botanic Garden is indistinguishable from a mature red oak until one spots the characteristic star-shaped leaves. Fall color is nothing short of phenomenal; multicolored is an understatement. It is not uncommon to find plants with bright yellow, maroon, and deep purple color that is long-lasting.

Sweetgum fall color ranges from yellow to purple.

Farther south, the tree is often referred to as the "monkey ball tree" because of its fruits, which resemble a medieval mace. As you can imagine, walking on sweetgum fruit barefoot can be excruciating; perhaps beneath a sweetgum is not the best spot for a picnic. Sun to part sun, average to wet soils, zones 6–9.

Sweetgum is a large, majestic tree with attractive foliage.

Tulip tree, *Liriodendron tulipifera*

While many gardeners south of the Mason-Dixon Line think of tulip trees (*Liriodendron tulipifera*) as weed trees, they grow quite differently in New England. In the South, with heavier soils and longer, warmer growing seasons, tulip tree grows so fast that the wood can be brittle and the trees can be messy, dropping branches during every windstorm. In New England, sandier soils and shorter, cooler summers contribute to slower growth and sturdier trees that make impressive specimens in the landscape.

Tulip tree is named both for its leaves (whose shape resembles a tulip) as well as for its fabulous yellow, orange, and green flowers that also resemble a tulip. The shape of its leaves is very unusual—there is not another species with leaves that even remotely resemble tulip tree's deep green foliage. The flowers appear in late spring and often appear high enough in the canopy that they can be tough to spot even if you're looking for them. Though the flowers are sometimes challenging to see,

The stately tulip tree

tulip tree has a consistent and striking upright, oval form that make it an attractive choice as a specimen.

Even in New England, tulip tree is faster growing than most of our other large canopy trees and will eventually reach heights of 70 to 120 feet, so proper siting is critical. If you have the space for a large tree, there are few better choices than tulip tree. Sun to part shade, average to moist soils, zones 4–9.

The leaves of tulip tree resemble the profile of a tulip flower.

Bayberry, *Morella (Myrica) caroliniensis*

Bayberry (*Morella caroliniensis*, formerly *Myrica pensylvanica*) is quite common along the coast of New England, but is usually restricted to high, dry ridgetops farther inland. It is a tough, dependable shrub that we often recommend people use in spots where they've had trouble establishing other shrubs because of dry soils.

The foliage of bayberry is broad, twisted, and matte green with a wonderful bay-like fragrance when brushed up against. The leaves can also be used in preparing soups or stews in the same manner as the typical culinary bay leaf—it would take an expert nose to tell the difference between this bayberry and bay laurel. The foliage is reluctantly deciduous, often holding on to its green color late into fall; the flip side is that bayberry can be later to leaf out in spring than many other deciduous shrubs.

Bayberry is dioecious, and the female plants produce an attractive light blue berry with a thin wax coating that was historically used to create bayberry candles. The amount of wax on each berry is so small that the thought of actually collecting enough to make a candle is laughable, but perhaps mixing some bayberry wax with traditional beeswax would be a viable option.

Because of its tolerance of poor, dry soils and salt, bayberry is a perfect parking lot plant. Combine it with butterfly milkweed (*Asclepias tuberosa*) and narrow-leaved mountain mint (*Pycnanthemum tenuifolium*), and you can turn areas typically barren of life into small biological hot spots for a tough but beautiful display for even the harshest location in the garden. Sun to part sun, average to dry soils, zones 4–7.

Bayberry
PHOTO BY WILLIAM CULLINA

Red mulberry

Red mulberry, *Morus rubra*

Red mulberry (*Morus rubra*) has an unfortunate reputation as a messy tree. Often, once people discover how tasty the deep red fruit is, the mess quickly disappears as the flavor is so excellent it seems a shame to let any go to waste. The berry looks and tastes similar to a blackberry but with a touch more sweetness and a little less tartness than the average blackberry. In a landscape with plenty of birds around, it is often a battle between you and the birds (especially the catbirds here at Garden in the Woods) to see who can get to them first.

Red mulberry's toothed leaves can range from unlobed to singly and doubly lobed, much like those of sassafras (*Sassafras albidum*). The form of the tree is similar to a mature crab apple or hawthorn, usually topping out at around thirty feet tall with a similar width.

Red mulberry can easily be confused with white mulberry (*M. alba*), a species native to China that is considered invasive in much of the Midwest. In New England, white mulberry does not currently meet the criteria for an invasive species, but it is at least an aggressive tree that should be avoided. Unfortunately, red and white mulberry hybridize regularly, and differentiating the species and hybrids can be very difficult. Sun to part shade, average to moist soils, zones 5–9.

Black gum, *Nyssa sylvatica*

There isn't a single plant that produces a better red fall color than black gum (*Nyssa sylvatica*), one of the most attractive native New England trees. Black gum grows naturally in wetlands throughout the region, but it also does well in average soils and can tolerate and thrive in poor, compacted soils.

Black gum has a distinctive form, with branches that regularly attach to its trunk at right angles, making it easy to identify even in winter. Its foliage, in addition to having incredible fall color, is consistently ornamental throughout the growing season thanks to its dark color and high gloss. Female trees produce a blue-black berry that is gobbled up by birds and edible to humans, though sour.

Although it may seem counterintuitive, like many wetland plants, black gum can tolerate low soil oxygen levels, making it a great choice

Black gum
PHOTO BY JACKIE DONNELLY

Black gum leaves have a wonderful glossy sheen.

for the urban landscape. When we examine soil a little more closely, however, we can see how this makes sense. In a wetland environment, water occupies the pore spaces that otherwise would be filled with air. In this sense, compacted soils mimic wetland soils, and are oxygen deprived. Plants like black gum that thrive in wetlands can often thrive in the poor, compacted, oxygen-deprived soils found in urban areas.

Black gum is best used as a specimen tree for vertical interest and fall color, growing narrowly to about sixty feet tall. It is notoriously difficult to transplant, owing to a strong taproot, so should only be planted as a young tree grown in a container, rather than field grown and balled-and-burlapped. Sun to part shade, wet to dry soils, zones 4–9.

Sourwood, *Oxydendrum arboreum*

Sourwood (*Oxydendrum arboreum*) comes a close second to black gum in the fall color category. It's hard to find a plant that can rival either of them in fall. A member of the heath family, sourwood is much less tolerant of poor soil conditions than black gum, growing best in the moist, humic soils preferred by rhododendrons and azaleas.

Another common name for sourwood is lily-of-the-valley tree, owing to its pendulous white flower clusters, which resemble the escaped European garden plant. Sourwood flowers grow on new wood in mid- to late summer, providing an interesting floral display and an important midsummer nectar source at a quiet time in the native plant garden. Once the flowers have gone, the maturing fruit hangs on through fall, almost giving the appearance of the plant still flowering while the foliage glows a brilliant red.

Because it is fairly nondescript when not in bloom, sourwood is easily lost in the spring and early summer landscape. For this reason, it

Sourwood

is often a welcome surprise to see one flowering in a place where you did not know it existed. In fact, at Garden in the Woods, two sourwoods are planted behind the tall shrub border along the edge of our swamp. It seems funny, but we all forget they are there until July or August, when they start to bloom, despite the impressive fall color display they reveal each and every year.

Sourwood is not a large tree—rounding out at about twenty-five feet tall, perhaps a little taller when crowded by other trees, and staying relatively narrow. The more sun they receive, the more vibrant the fall color. Sun to part shade, moist to average soil, zones 5–9.

Sourwood is a great small tree for any garden.

Ninebark, *Physocarpus opulifolius*

There are dozens of great multistemmed flowering shrubs available for New England gardeners. Few of them boast as long a season of interest as ninebark (*Physocarpus opulifolius*). From spring flowers to unusually colorful fruit and striking, exfoliating bark, ninebark offers true four-season interest as well as great support for pollinators. Ninebark also offers perhaps the best native alternative to Japanese barberry (*Berberis thunbergii*), a beautiful but terribly invasive species imported from Asia. Thanks to a couple of purple-leaved selections like Diablo® and Coppertina®, those seeking an attractive shrub with purple leaves that can be used in formal landscapes can opt for ninebark instead of barberry.

Ninebark's ornamental season starts with its late spring flowers, which are simple, white, and arranged in spherical clusters. As a member of the rose family, ninebark's individual flowers resemble those of other species found here, like three-toothed cinquefoil (*Sibbaldiopsis tridentata*) and chokeberry. Flowers are followed by colorful reddish clusters

Ninebark
PHOTO BY WILLIAM CULLINA

of fruit that can persist into winter. Ninebark is underappreciated for its fruit display; in fact, the plant often is sheared to give it a neater look, unfortunately cutting off both flowers and fruit in many cases.

Its leaves are simple, normally with three lobes and a serrated edge. Purple-leaved forms, as mentioned previously, are a suitable replacement for the purple-leaved forms of Japanese barberry; however, the fruits are often overwhelmed and difficult to appreciate against the darker foliage of these cultivars. For winter interest, ninebark offers incredibly attractive bark. Where the papery outer bark peels off, it leaves behind a rich, cinnamon-colored inner bark. Ninebark can reach ten to twelve feet in height. As it matures, it becomes more vase-shaped and stems lose vigor. Gardeners would be wise to thin it periodically, removing the oldest, largest stems and helping the shrub to maintain its vigor. Sun to part shade, average to dry soils, zones 3–8.

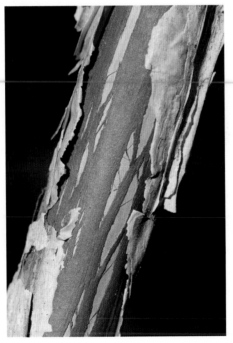

Ninebark stems become more attractive with age.

Cherry and plum, *Prunus* spp.

Prunus is a diverse genus in New England that includes four different plums and five different cherries (depending on whose naming you follow). If you're looking for ecological value, any of the species listed here are of great value, with black cherry (*Prunus serotina*) making our top ten woodies list.

Of the three species discussed, black cherry is the only real tree among them. They usually grow from twenty-five to fifty feet tall, but every now and again you can find an ancient specimen reaching heights of one hundred feet. White flowers coat the branches in late spring,

Black cherry

followed by edible cherries. The flavor can range from one individual to the next, but many trees produce wonderfully flavored cherries that are enjoyed by humans as much as the local bird populations. Though sweet, the cherries also have an inherent tartness that many edibles enthusiasts claim gives them a richer flavor than store-bought varieties. Sun to part sun, dry to moist soils, zones 3–9.

Choke cherry (*P. virginiana*) is both known and unknown. Many people are familiar with the species by name but couldn't pick it out of a lineup, and we think it deserves much more recognition than it gets. This is a shrubby species, often staying under fifteen feet but capable of reaching thirty feet when the conditions are right. Masses of fragrant white flowers are followed by edible yet unpalatable cherries that birds find irresistible. There is some range of decent fall color as well, usually leaning in the yellow or red direction. Choke cherry is a suckering shrub that will form a colony when space allows. It is controllable, but it's better to plant it somewhere where you're looking for a suckering, colonizing shrub. Sun to part shade, dry to average soils, zones 2–7.

Beach plum (*P. maritima*) is well-known in coastal areas but is significantly less common as you move inland. It thrives in sandy soils under the blazing sun and shrugs off salt spray without difficulty. If you have the right area in which to plant a beach plum (sunny and well drained), don't miss the opportunity—the flowers are almost as beautiful as the plums are tasty. That being said, this is a plant for sunny, dry sites and will not perform well in other conditions. Sun, dry to average soils, zones 4–8.

Oak, *Quercus* spp.

There are more than a dozen species of oak native to New England, ranging from the regal white oak (*Quercus alba*) to the shrubby scrub oak (*Q. ilicifolia*) and the sculptural post oak (*Q. stellata*). Oaks are likely the single biggest supporter of native wildlife, supporting hundreds of native lepidopteran (moth and butterfly) and, in turn, native bird species. Not every oak is garden worthy, but many of them have attributes that make them attractive to the native plant enthusiast.

White oak (*Q. alba*) is easily the most majestic New England oak. It is incredibly long-lived and has a characteristic broad, spreading form that makes it identifiable from one hundred yards away. White oak can grow to heights of eighty or more feet, and is often nearly as wide as it is tall, so giving it enough space to spread out is critical. In addition to its sheer size, white oak has attractive leaves with rounded lobes. Newly emerging leaves are a brilliant red in spring, mirroring the color of this tree's fall foliage. Sun to light shade, average to dry soils, zones 3–9.

Scarlet oak (*Q. coccinea*) is grown primarily for its fall color, a tremendous scarlet red. Like most oaks, scarlet oak's fall foliage is long-lasting, persisting for weeks when the weather cooperates. It is an upland species, intolerant of poor drainage and, with a typical oak taproot, can be difficult to transplant except when young. In addition to its fall foliage, scarlet oak's leaves are quite distinctive, with deep sinuses and sharply pointed lobes. Viewed from the right angle, the sinuses appear to outline the letter "c," a characteristic that reminds every horticulture student studying plant identification and memorizing Latin names of its species name, "coccinea." Sun to light shade, average to dry soils, zones 4–8.

Pin oak (*Q. palustris*) is a common street tree, although due to its characteristic form, it's probably the worst oak one could choose to plant anywhere but an open field. Its prevalence as a common landscape tree owes more to its lack of a taproot and ease of transplanting than its merits as a street tree. Pin oak has a strong central leader and an upright, oval form. Its branches grow off the main trunk in three distinct planes. Branches toward the top point strongly upward, branches in the mid-plane attach at right angles and extend straight out, perpendicular to the trunk, and branches in the lower plane seem to point almost straight downward, at about a 45-degree angle to the trunk. It is these lower branches that make pin oak problematic as a street tree. Rather than committing to the frequent pruning necessary to limb this tree up and away from traffic, we'd recommend any other oak as a better street tree. Native to floodplains, pin oak is tolerant of moist soils. Sun to light shade, average to moist soils, zones 4–8.

Red oak (*Q. rubra*) is a fast-growing and dominant tree species throughout much of New England, especially in the southern states. Its leaves are not quite as attractive as those of either scarlet or white oak, and its fall color is more muted. But red oak bark is narrowly fissured or cracked, revealing a distinct red color that seems to be just below the bark surface. When it rains, the color of the fissures is more pronounced, whether because the rest of the bark becomes darker or the reddish color becomes brighter. Red oak is more of a bottomland species, preferring moister soils than scarlet oak, but also has a taproot and is difficult to transplant. Perhaps red oak's greatest attribute is its growth rate, which is quite a bit faster than that of white oak or scarlet oak. Sun to light shade, average soils, zones 3–8.

Red oak bark

Rosebay and azalea, *Rhododendron* spp.

Native rhododendrons can be divided into two distinct categories—broad-leaved evergreens like great rosebay (*Rhododendron maximum*) and Labrador tea (*R. groenlandicum*), and multistemmed, deciduous azaleas like pinxterbloom azalea (*R. periclymenoides*) or early azalea (*R. prinophyllum*). Many of them are great garden plants, but often they are overlooked and underused in the landscape in favor of their Asian counterparts. Three of the best choices for the garden follow, in order of bloom time.

Our native deciduous azaleas put on quite a show in spring, often blooming before new leaves unfurl in spring. Pinxterbloom azalea is one of the earliest to flower, opening in late April to reveal fragrant, light to dark pink blossoms on otherwise naked stems. When happy, pinxterbloom azalea will spread to form a small patch of suckering stems to about six feet in height. Part sun to shade, moist to average soils, zones 4–8.

Clammy or swamp azalea (*R. viscosum*) flowers later than pinxterbloom, usually blooming in early summer in New England, from late June into July. Because its flowers open after it leaves unfurl, the floral display is not quite as dramatic as that of the earlier blooming azaleas, but what it lacks in visual drama, swamp azalea makes up for with an overpowering, spicy-sweet fragrance. Part sun to shade, moist to average soils, zones 4–9.

Great rosebay, also known simply as "rhody max," is a massive evergreen shrub with large, deep green leaves that are roughly four or five times longer than wide. In the wild, great rosebay is found in moist soils, but in cultivation, it can handle drier soils without difficulty. Like most rhododendrons, great rosebay is happiest in shade, and though tolerant of full sun, it appears to be more susceptible to damage from black vine weevil when exposed to too much sun. Flowers are light pink to white, opening in late June and blooming through July. Part shade to shade, average to moist soils, zones 3–8.

Great rosebay flowers

Fragrant sumac

Sumac, *Rhus* spp.

Collectively, the sumacs (*Rhus* spp.) have some of the most spectacular fall color of any native New England plants. Although some sumacs have a (well-deserved) reputation as garden thugs, their incredible fall display makes including at least one sumac in every New England garden a must.

Fragrant sumac (*Rhus aromatica*) is our top recommendation for most garden uses. While it is a multistemmed, colonizing shrub like many of its cousins, it is much slower growing, and fairly easy to control even in a formal garden. The flowers are interesting at best and the fruits are showy if inconsistent, but the fall color is remarkable and reason enough to include it in your garden. The color ranges from yellow to orange to red on plants that reach about four to six feet in height. A very popular cultivar called *R. aromatica* 'Gro-Low' tops out at around two feet tall and has glossier foliage than the natural species. Sun to part shade, dry to average soils, zones 4–9.

Staghorn sumac (*R. typhina*) is the most common species in much of New England and ranges in size from six to eight feet on average, but can reach heights of twelve feet commonly and eighteen feet occasionally. In the garden, cutting back the stems every few years keeps the plants shorter in stature and a little neater. Staghorn sumac consistently produces edible fruit each year that is considered tastier than the fruit of other sumacs. Collect fruits when they are bright red and steep them in warm (not hot) water until flavorful. The resulting "rhus juice" is sweet yet tangy and makes for an excellent drink to enjoy either on its own or mixed into cocktails. Fall color is a deep and vibrant red and puts the invasive burning bush (*Euonymous alatus*) to shame. Sun to part shade, dry to average soils, zones 4–8.

Winged sumac (*R. copallinum*) is a closely related species that is more common in coastal New England. The foliage has a wonderful shine to the leaves that gives it its secondary common name, "shining sumac." Sun to part shade, dry to average soils, zones 4–9.

Carolina rose, *Rosa carolina*

There was some discussion as whether or not to include roses in this book, as most folks either love them or hate them. Those folks who love roses often deal with marginally hardy, non-native species complete with a variety of disease and insect problems that they are happy to put up with for the fabulous flowers produced in the summer months. Our native roses are a different story altogether. They will not produce the giant flowers found in the florist's shop, but they also need next to no care from the gardener.

Carolina rose (*Rosa carolina*) is a drought-tolerant, sun-loving species with small pink flowers that start out deep pink and fade to a lighter hue after a few days. The stems are covered in small, glossy leaves that catch the sun nicely, making this rose attractive even before it blooms. The hips that follow the flowers are a deep crimson red that keep Carolina rose looking good until fall kicks in and the leaves change to a rich red.

Carolina rose has ample wildlife value, from flowers and fruits to leaves that are important host sites for numerous native caterpillars. Sun to part shade, dry to average soils, zones 4–9.

Carolina rose

Flowering raspberry has both pleasant pink flowers and tasty fruit.

Raspberry, *Rubus* spp.

In New England, we find nearly thirty native species of blackberries and raspberries in the genus *Rubus*. For edible plants, our top choices are blackberry (*Rubus alleghaniensis*), red raspberry (*R. idaeus*), and black raspberry (*R. occidentalis*). In terms of flavor, red raspberry is considered the sweetest of the lot, while blackberry is the tartest; each of them has a flavor similar to the next but unique enough to differentiate it from its cousins. For some reason, blackberries and raspberries do not fruit well every year, so the smart gardener would be wise to plant all three species to ensure a good fruit set each year. Sun to part shade, dry to moist soils, zones 3–8.

Your imagination is all that restricts your use of blackberries and raspberries. Of course, they are wonderful eaten fresh, but they also make great preserves, are great baked with fish or chicken, are an interesting addition to salsas and a tasty flavor for "rhus juice," ginger beer, and vodka in a Pink Monkey cocktail.

Flowering raspberry (*R. odoratus*) is different from the others in the sense that, while the fruit is just as edible, if a little less flavorful, it is far more ornamental. The leaves of flowering raspberry are significantly larger than those of other raspberries and roughly star-shaped. Large flowers emerge from dark pink buds that open to reveal lighter pink flowers. The stems are protected by hairs, making them a little less threatening than the imposing thorns covering the stems of many other raspberries and blackberries. Flowering raspberry also tolerates light shade better than the other species. Don't just plant an edible garden, plant a garden full of edible and ornamentals! Sun to part shade, average to moist soils, zones 4–6.

Elderberry, *Sambucus nigra* and *Sambucus racemosa*

Two distinct species of elderberry exist in New England. Black elderberry (*Sambucus nigra*, formerly *S. canadensis*) is a tall, upright flowering shrub that can be a little gangly and awkward but has remarkable white flowers in early summer, followed by dark, edible (once processed) fruits. Red elderberry (*S. racemosa*) is somewhat smaller in stature than black elderberry and perhaps a slightly better garden plant than its cousin, owing to its larger and more colorful red fruit.

Black elderberry grows to about ten feet in height. It's a very common roadside plant, occurring naturally in sunny, moist, forested edges. Fairly nondescript until its flowers appear in midsummer, black elderberry puts on quite a floral display. Large, flat-topped clusters of brilliant white flowers appear at the tops of this plant's fairly brittle stems. Immediately after flowering, edible black fruits appear, often weighing branches down until they touch the ground. Leaves are compound, with five to seven leaflets. Black elderberry is happiest in full sun, with adequate moisture. Due to its informal habit and brittle stems that frequently break under the weight of its heavy fruit set, we recommend using this one in masses, rather than as a single specimen shrub. Sun to part shade, moist to wet soils, zones 4–9.

Red elderberry is quite similar to black elderberry. It is slightly shorter in stature when mature and flowers in spring, a few weeks earlier than black elderberry. Flowers are followed by brilliant red fruit that are enjoyed by wildlife. Sun to part shade, moist to wet soils, zones 3–7.

Black elderberry

Sassafras

Sassafras, *Sassafras albidum*

It's hard to imagine why sassafras (*Sassafras albidum*) isn't used more often. Although it can be hard to use in small spaces, it's a tough tree with some outstanding ornamental attributes and it seems a shame not to see it in more gardens. Sassafras has multiple leaf shapes—ranging from unlobed to single lobed to double lobed. The single-lobed leaves resemble a small child's mitten, while the double-lobed leaves look like the footprint of a *Tyrannosaurus rex*. Historically, its roots were harvested to make a variety of medicines; at one point, the roots were so popular that an entire sassafras market grew and thrived on Cape Cod and Martha's Vineyard, where these plants are very common. The young twigs make a very tasty tea, and the leaves can be dried and ground and added to soups as a thickening agent.

By far the best attribute of sassafras is its fall color, which can be truly breathtaking. It's rare that it is any single color, instead maturing into a kaleidoscope of reds, oranges, and yellows. The tree's form is suckering, forming a colony of upright stems over time, which is why it can be difficult to work into small landscapes. Sassafras also exhibits something called "sympodial branching," which gives mature trees a bit of a zigzag appearance. Despite its suckering habit, sassafras makes a great shade tree for the front lawn, where emerging suckers can simply be run over with the lawnmower to maintain it as a single-stemmed specimen. We also love to let a young patch of sassafras grow up and then cut a path into the middle of it. Though it will take maintaining, you've just built yourself an outdoor room, complete with living walls, that just asks for a bench (or fort) where you can sit and view the myriad bird species that will visit your patch. Sassafras is the secondary host for the spicebush swallowtail caterpillar. Sun to part shade, dry to moist soils, zones 4–9.

Three-toothed cinquefoil, *Sibbaldiopsis* (*Potentilla*) *tridentata*

A frequently overlooked little shrub, three-toothed cinquefoil (*Sibbaldiopsis tridentata*) is one of those really tough plants for tough places that provide year-round interest. Similar to bearberry (*Arctostaphylos uva-ursi*) in that it has four seasons of interest, three-toothed cinquefoil may be slightly less finicky about its site conditions, but it still requires the right site with excellent drainage to be happy.

Three-toothed cinquefoil is a member of the rose family and produces characteristic white flowers in spring that resemble those of serviceberry. Its best ornamental attribute has to be its foliage—glossy, evergreen, three-lobed leaves that turn burgundy in fall. Like bearberry, three-toothed cinquefoil is quite short, growing only to about three or four inches in height, but spreads quite vigorously. It is a near-perfect groundcover for exposed, dry, sandy soils, where it can form a thick mat and act as a great living mulch, keeping other plants and weeds at bay.

If not growing in full sun, three-toothed cinquefoil can eventually start to peter out, but because of its tolerance of poor soils and sun exposure, it makes a great roadside or parking lot plant. Flowers emerge in late spring, followed by dry fruits that easily spread seed. After its initial flowering period, it will continue to flower sporadically for several weeks. Three-toothed cinquefoil is often found growing in cracks and crevices in alpine or subalpine zones, making it a sought-after rock garden plant. Full sun, average to dry, well-drained soils, zones 2–7.

Three-toothed cinquefoil is a tough but attractive groundcover.

Steeplebush

Steeplebush, *Spiraea tomentosa*

Steeplebush (*Spiraea tomentosa*) is usually found in moist meadows and wetland edges in the wild, but in garden settings it is quite drought tolerant once established. Light to bright pink spiked flowers top tall stems that point skyward during the summer months. The flowers resemble lilac (*Syringa vulgaris*) or butterfly bush (*Buddleia davidii*), and unlike those two non-native species, steeplebush not only feeds adult butterflies but also provides host sites for their caterpillars.

This plant (as well as a few others such as red-twig dogwood [*Swida sericea*] and smooth hydrangea [*Hydrangea arborescens*]) is one of a few woody shrubs that can be cut back to the ground without damaging the plant, making it a great choice as a foundation planting or anywhere else where snow damage is a concern. In addition to its value as a garden ornamental, steeplebush works well in rain gardens and bioswales, where it can be combined with plants like rose milkweed (*Asclepias incarnata*), and Joe-Pye weed to slow and filter stormwater. Sun to part shade, dry to moist soils, zones 3–8.

Meadowsweet (*S. latifolia*) is a closely related plant that can often be found in similar environments, with an upland variety (var. *latifolia*) and a wetland variety (var. *alba*). It differs mainly in the color of its flowers, which start out a nice pure white before fading to brown with maturity. Meadowsweet is a fine plant, but we prefer steeplebush for the color of its blooms. Sun to part shade, dry to average (for var. *latifolia*), average to moist (for var. *alba*), zones 3–8.

Red-twig dogwood, *Swida (Cornus) sericea*

There are few plants that look better in winter than red-twig dogwood (*Swida sericea*). While there are a number of woody plants whose unique forms lend interest to the winter landscape, none of them rival the color of red-twig dogwood. The red stems appear even more vibrant against a backdrop of snow, making this the only native shrub that we can claim looks better in winter than at any other time of year.

Like smooth hydrangea (*Hydrangea arborescens*) and steeplebush (*Spiraea tomentosa*), red-twig dogwood can be cut back to the ground as you might prune a perennial, making it a good choice for under eves or any other place where falling snow can be damaging. Even if this is not necessary, we recommend thinning red-twig dogwood every three years or so, removing the oldest stems as the newer stems are significantly more colorful.

In addition to the colorful stems, red-twig dogwood has a white flower and white berries that appear in late spring and summer, respectively. While neither the flower nor the fruit is nearly as showy as the winter stems, they are nonetheless nice to look at, and the birds most certainly enjoy the berries. The leaves are important host sites for native caterpillars. Despite their preference for moist soils, red-twig dogwoods are happy in average garden soils and become quite drought tolerant once established. Sun to part shade, dry to moist soils, zones 2–7.

There is a closely related species—smooth dogwood (*S. amomum*)—that seems to be more common in the wild in New England. The form is a little wilder than that of red-twig dogwood, and the stems are usually closer to maroon than bright red. Despite this, it is still a beautiful plant and one worth exploring if you've already fallen in love with red-twig dogwood. Sun to part shade, average to moist soils, zones 4–8.

Red-twig dogwood stems brighten the winter garden.

Blueberry, *Vaccinium* spp.

Vaccinium is a diverse genus in New England that includes the well-known highbush (*V. corymbusum*) and lowbush blueberries (*V. angustifolium*) mentioned here as well as a slew of lesser-known blueberries, three different cranberries, and deerberry (*V. stamineum*).

As tasty as blueberries are, it is somewhat unfortunate that when we think of the plants, we tend to restrict them to our edible gardens. The berries are amazingly tasty and are indeed reason enough to plant them, but blueberries have a lot more to offer than just a tasty snack.

Blueberries are one of the best shrubs to plant in support of local wildlife—and it may not be for the reason you think. As important as the berries are for birds, and as much as the bees love the flowers, it is the leaves, which act as host sites for native caterpillars, that puts blueberries at the top of the list. Bumblebees have developed a special strategy for acquiring the pollen of blueberries (and other related species); they land on the flowers and rapidly vibrate their wings to loosen the pollen within. Buzz pollination is one of the main reasons that native bees are so important to our ecosystem, as the European honeybee is unable to perform this unique feat.

In addition to the edible and ecological value of blueberries, blueberries are incredibly beautiful. White (sometimes tinged pink) flowers appear in early spring, followed by the edible blue fruit in summer. The flowers and berries are attractive, but the fall color is what really makes blueberry a prized ornamental plant. When grown in full sun, the foliage turns such a vibrant red that one wonders why anyone would ever plant the invasive burning bush (*Euonymus alatus*).

Lowbush blueberry grows only to about twelve inches tall, is tolerant of extremely dry soils, and will grow anywhere, from full sun to dense shade. In shade, flower and fruit set will be sparse, but lowbush blueberry's value as a groundcover is good reason to plant it even in deep shade under pines and hemlocks. Sun to shade, average to dry soils, zones 3–8.

Highbush blueberry is quite drought tolerant once established but prefers moist to wet soils. In the wild, it's not uncommon to find highbush blueberry growing in standing water, and for optimal fruit production, you'll want to plant it in a sunny, moist area. Sun to part sun, wet to average soils, zones 3–8. Acidic soils are necessary for both species.

Few things are as quintessentially New England as lowbush blueberry in fall.
PHOTO COURTESY OF NATIVESCAPESMA

Viburnum, *Viburnum* spp.

Though there are plenty of other genera in New England that contain more species than *Viburnum*, there are few other genera that include as many useful garden plants. While it's impossible to cover them all, the following short list represents some of the best choices for New England gardens.

While many viburnums are easy to grow, even for the beginning gardener, hobblebush (*V. lantanoides*) can be quite difficult, especially in southern New England. If you can get it established, however, hobblebush could easily be considered the most beautiful of all the native viburnums. The inflorescence is comprised of both small fertile flowers and large sterile flowers, followed by blue fruits that are both attractive and tasty. Fall color is incredible, often ranging from red to yellow to purple—all on a single shrub. Shade, average soils, zones 4–6.

There are few better shrubs for dry shade and acid soils than maple-leaved viburnum (*V. acerifolium*). Its flowers are small but numerous, and the blue fruits that follow are an added bonus. But the real showy season for maple-leaved viburnum is fall, when its foliage turns bright red or a brilliant mix of red and purple. Sun to shade, average to dry soils, zones 3–9.

Next to hobblebush, perhaps the showiest native viburnum is witherod, or possum haw viburnum (*V. nudum*). The species is split into two botanical varieties, both of which are native to New England. The northern variety, *V. nudum* var. *cassinoides*, is slightly more cold tolerant and the better choice for northern New England gardeners. The southern variety, *V. nudum* var. *nudum*, is slightly more ornamental, with a wonderful gloss to its leaves. The fruit display on both varieties is spectacular, showier than that of any other viburnum (and perhaps most other native shrubs). Witherod has green berries that mature to red before finally turning blue, like many of the viburnums. Unlike many of the others, however, there is a period of time when both the red and blue berries are present, appearing almost like a small fireworks display. As the berries mature to blue, the foliage turns vibrant red, lending a wonderful contrast to the display. Sun to part shade, average to wet soils, zones 3–9.

American cranberry bush

For sunny, moist areas, cranberry bush (*V. opulus*) is often the best choice. The flowers are just as showy as those of hobblebush, and the fruits that follow are bright red and easily the best choice for human consumption. They taste remarkably similar to cranberries but are much juicier.

Unfortunately, several native viburnum species are now heavily damaged by an introduced insect pest called viburnum leaf beetle. Cranberry bush and arrowwood viburnum (*V. dentatum*) are most susceptible. If you are unsure whether viburnum leaf beetle exists in your area, be careful when choosing either of these plants—viburnum leaf beetle damage can be devastating and will kill a shrub over time. Sun to part sun, average to dry soils, zones 4–9.

Ferns, Grasses, and Sedges

If herbaceous perennials are eye-popping and often dramatic in bloom, and trees and shrubs provide structure and year-round interest, many of the plants in this chapter are understated and dignified. Ferns, ancient relics of the plant world that don't even produce flowers, are great fillers in a perennial garden, or make outstanding groundcovers when a quiet, low-maintenance space is desirable. Grasses and sedges are a versatile group of plants that often provides fine texture, in contrast with many of the plants in the preceding chapters. The plants in this chapter also offer some of the best alternatives to the traditional American lawn that we find in the native plant palette.

Maidenhair fern, *Adiantum pedatum*

When people go from passing interest to complete obsession with ferns, it is often thanks to maidenhair fern (*Adiantum pedatum*) and its undeniably unique branching fronds (fern leaves) resting atop a wiry black stem. Because of its unique form and its growth habit, maidenhair fern can be used either as a specimen or in large sweeps. In sweeps, it forms a lush, soft carpet of fine-textured foliage that can provide textural contrast for other low-growing perennials or adorn the feet of taller perennials and shrubs. As a specimen, maidenhair's architectural fronds are exquisite, and one can easily get lost following the spiraling, bisected fronds with the eye.

Surround benches or corners of the garden with clumps of maidenhair fern to soften the aesthetic. It works well adorning the edge of a trail and even better on slopes, where the fronds hide the stems when viewed from above and contrast them wonderfully when viewed from below.

Maidenhair fern

Though not as easy to grow as lady fern (*Athyrium angustum*) or as fast growing as most of the wood ferns (*Dryopteris* spp.), maidenhair fern is nonetheless easy to grow if given the correct conditions. While it is fairly tough when established and easy enough to transplant, it does prefer rich, moist soils and can struggle if not sited properly. Often found in higher pH soils in the wild, maidenhair fern does perfectly well in the standard acidic soils of most New England gardens. Part shade to shade, average to moist soils, zones 2–9.

Maidenhair fern works well as a specimen or en masse.

Big bluestem, *Andropogon gerardii*, and bushy bluestem, *Andropogon glomeratus*

New England native grass species differ greatly from the European species that dominate most roadside meadows in our area. When you look upon a native meadow, you see a landscape dominated by grass species with a great variety of herbaceous perennials mixed in among the grasses. Conversely, those areas dominated by the European species first brought over by early settlers often lack herbaceous perennials completely. The distinction becomes evident once you start looking at how the grasses differ. Our native species are almost entirely clumping species, which may appear as a solid mass when first viewed, but when looking at the base of the grass, you can see that all stems emerge from a central root system. The European species are mainly rhizomatous, and this is a major difference. Our native meadow perennials can take full advantage of this spacing, often dropping seed or spreading rhizomes of their own into the spaces in between native grasses.

Andropogon is a perfect example of this difference, and the difference in habitat provided to our native bees and ground-nesting birds is obvious when you begin noticing these distinctions. There are two major species in the horticultural trade. Big bluestem (*A. gerardii*) is the grass of choice when one is looking for a tall species that can range from moist to dry sites and will never flop over in windy sites like many other species of grasses. Big bluestem starts out as a handsome blue-tinged grass that matures into wonderful shades of red, orange, and brown as late summer turns to fall. Sun, average to dry soils, zones 4–9.

Bushy bluestem (*A. glomeratus*) is the unsung hero of the genus and best planted in moist to wet sites. This might be why *A. gerardii* is more commonly used, but when the site is right, bushy bluestem is an exquisite specimen. Blue-tinged stems are topped with bushy flowers that are rich brown at the base and a showy silvery-white on top. The flowers show up beautifully against the early season foliage, and the entire effect becomes more pronounced as the foliage matures into its fall glory. If you can find the right spot for bushy bluestem, you will not regret including it in your garden! Sun, average to wet soils, zones 5–9.

Bushy bluestem
PHOTO BY WILLIAM CULLINA

Lady fern, *Athyrium angustum*

Lady fern (*Athyrium angustum*) is one of those native plants that look delicate and difficult to grow but are really the exact opposite. Whether in dense shade to part sun, lady fern is happy enough just about anywhere that gets adequate moisture. In periods of drought, lady fern might die back to the ground but it will resprout when moisture returns. This trick is especially useful if you happen to grow *A. angustum* 'Lady in Red,' a red-stemmed form, since the color is most vibrant on new foliage. It's advisable to cut this fern back halfway through the season to force a new flush of growth and see that bright red emerge again later in summer.

The color of the rachis (stem) ranges between individual plants, and it is not uncommon to see red-stemmed plants labeled as *A. angustum* var. *rubrum* in the trade, although this is not considered a true botanical form. 'Lady in Red' is a New England Wild Flower Society introduction discovered in Vermont by a longtime member, photographer John Lynch.

'Lady in Red' fern
PHOTO BY WILLIAM CULLINA

A great use for lady fern is to plant small clusters of three to seven plants among large sweeps of shorter groundcovers. For example, at Garden in the Woods, we planted small clusters of 'Lady in Red' among large sweeps of phlox and foamflower (*Tiarella cordifolia* var. *cordifolia*). This upright and colorful element adds summer intrigue to an otherwise spring-focused display. Part shade to shade, average to moist soils, zones 2–9.

An emerging lady fern fiddlehead

Pennsylvania sedge is a nearly perfect lawn alternative for dry shade.

Pennsylvania sedge, *Carex pensylvanica*, and plantain sedge, *Carex plantaginea*

This normally surprises people, but the sedges are some of the top plants for pollinators in New England, supporting dozens of moth and butterfly species. They also happen to be fantastic lawn alternatives, especially for dry shade. Unusual when compared to many other sedge species, Pennsylvania sedge (*Carex pensylvanica*) spreads by sending out shallow rhizomes and forming a dense mat over time that can look from a distance like a traditional turfgrass lawn. Unlike traditional turfgrass lawns, however, this sedge does not require irrigation, only needs to be mowed once per year (if at all), and grows perfectly well in places where most turfgrass lawns really struggle.

Pennsylvania sedge grows naturally in the understory of a dry oak forest, in dry, acidic soils and shade. Taken out of this context, it does perfectly well when given richer soils and a little more sunlight. It has fine-textured, deep green foliage that will grow to about ten inches in height if left unmowed, normally gently bending over rather than standing upright, resulting in an effective height in the garden of about six inches. Where it differs from traditional turfgrass species is in its growth cycle. Sedges send out a single flush of growth in spring, and by early summer have largely stopped growing for the year. When timed properly, a single mowing at about the middle of June is all that is necessary to keep Pennsylvania sedge at a comfortable four or five inches in height for the rest of the year. At Garden in the Woods, we have a small "sedge lawn" that to the casual observer looks just like a traditional Kentucky bluegrass lawn. Sun to shade, average to dry soils, zones 3–8.

A related sedge with a very different appearance is plantain sedge (*C. plantaginea*). With much broader foliage and a distinctly clumping growth habit, plantain sedge works best as an accent plant, where its bright green foliage can provide a bright spark in a shady perennial garden. Plantain sedge grows to about ten inches in height and width, and features flowers in spring that are quite beautiful in their own way, if more structural than flashy. Part sun to shade, moist soils, zones 4–8.

Wood fern, *Dryopteris* spp.

Wood ferns (*Dryopteris* spp.) are a diverse group ranging from the fragrant wood fern (*D. fragrans*), found almost exclusively on cliffs in the northern New England states, to the spinulose wood fern (*D. carthusiana*), which is present in every single county in New England. Ironically, one of New England's rarer species is also one of the easiest to use in the garden. Goldie's wood fern (*D. goldiana*) is considered uncommon or rare in Connecticut, Massachusetts, and Maine, where it is found most often in high pH soils. In the garden, it is an easygoing plant that grows to about three or four feet tall with a nice tight clumping form. At Garden in the Woods, we like to intersperse it among shorter woodland perennials, using it as a vertical accent. Part shade to shade, average to moist soils, zones 3–8.

Another great wood fern is the intermediate fern (*D. intermedia*), which has a soft, almost delicate appearance thanks to its lacey foliage. Smaller in stature, it is best used more as a filler or in mass plantings than as a specimen like Goldie's fern. Intermediate fern does not spread vigorously, and so makes a good choice to fill an area without taking over a whole section of the garden. Part shade to shade, dry to moist soils, zones 3–8.

Marginal wood fern (*D. marginalis*) boasts a number of advantages over its relatives. For one thing, it's incredibly easy to grow. The fronds are only twice cut and thus have a stronger texture when compared to intermediate fern. This is one of the shadiest, most acid- and drought-tolerant ferns in New England. If you want ferns in an area where they've failed in the past, marginal fern is a good one to try. Part shade to shade, dry to moist soils, zones 3–8.

Goldie's wood fern

The fertile fronds of fiddlehead fern persist through winter.

Fiddlehead fern, *Matteuccia struthiopteris*

Of all the ferns native to New England, fiddlehead fern (*Matteuccia struthiopteris*) is the only one recommended for eating. Because identifying ferns in the wild can be difficult, even for experts, and the fiddleheads, a term that describes the newly emerged and expanding fronds on all ferns, lose flavor quickly after harvest, it's best to grow these in your garden rather than try to wild-forage. Harvest fiddleheads in early spring, and be sure to both boil (to remove tannins) and then pan-fry (to degrade the enzyme thiaminase) to cook them properly. Serve fiddleheads with some browned butter, lemon zest, salt, and pepper and await the praise.

In addition to their use in the kitchen, fiddlehead fern is a fabulous plant for the landscape when the conditions are right. In time, it will spread with some vigor and should be planted in an area where it has room to spread and won't impact more delicate plants. It's hard to describe the impact of a fiddlehead fern in the garden. It is a tall, statuesque plant with deep green fronds until late summer, when it starts to go dormant. Perhaps its most interesting ornamental feature is the upright fertile frond that outlasts the others' foliage and persists through winter, adding a delicate complexity to the winter landscape. As with many of the other native ferns, there is an argument to be made for this fern being the showiest in early spring. The emerging fiddleheads are a rich, deep green and are covered in large, brown, paper-like scales that drop off as the fronds mature.

A spreading, colonizing plant that is happy in moist soils, fiddlehead fern is a great choice for streambanks or moist trail edges, where it not only looks great but plays an important role in stabilizing soil. Sun to shade, average to moist soils, zones 2–8.

Long beech fern, *Phegopteris connectilis*

Long beech fern (*Phegopteris connectilis*) is a somewhat new fern for us, and yet in the short time that we've used it, this fern has quickly risen to the top of our favorite plants list. This is a patch-forming species in the manner of hay-scented fern (*Dennstaedtia punctilobula*) though without the immense vigor of hay-scented. A thick patch of the stuff has such a lush appearance that the fern can stand alone without looking boring at all. It usually tops out at around twelve to sixteen inches, making it excellent for lining the edges of paths or framing other patch-forming species. That being said, a thick chunk of long beech fern combined with larger clumping species such as King Solomon's seal (*Polygonatum biflorum*) or blue cohosh (*Caulophyllum thalictroides*) shooting through it can create a simple yet elegant woodland scene that just asks for a bench, a good book, and a couple of hours to simply sit and enjoy.

Long beech fern

Despite its ability to fill an area, long beech fern tends to play well with others. At Garden in the Woods, we've started planting it not only with strong clumping species but also with more delicate ones such as bloodroot (*Sanguinaria canadensis*) and trillium. The rachis tends to grow up for only a few inches before it begins to nod over, allowing the fronds to sit parallel to the ground instead of standing up straight like most other ferns. Not only does this add a touch of unique ornamental character to the fern, but it also means that it produces dense shade, and once a patch is established, it works incredibly well as a living mulch, effectively keeping weeds at bay.

A related species, broad beech fern (*P. hexagonoptera*), grows faster and larger than its more diminutive cousin. It can be used where a dense, patch-forming fern is desired, but broad beech fern has coarser texture and lacks the delicate appearance of its smaller cousin, long beech fern. Part shade to shade, average to moist soils, zones 2–7.

Christmas fern, *Polystichum acrostichoides*

Good evergreen foliage is invaluable in the garden, and Christmas fern (*Polystichum acrostichoides*) provides not only year-round interest with its glossy green leaves, but also beautiful early spring emergence thanks to a stunning fiddlehead. During winters with little snow cover, the previous season's fronds look pretty tattered by spring. Whether or not to cut them back is a point of debate among many gardeners. On the one hand, it's a pity to lose the greenery at a time when our gardens can look pretty bare; on the other hand, the newly emerging fiddleheads are perhaps slightly more attractive without last year's foliage obscuring them. We recommend experimenting before deciding for yourself whether to cut them back or not.

Christmas fern

Christmas fern works well either as a stand-alone clump in amongst a patch of lower-growing species or when planted in large drifts in a mixed perennial border. Combine it with other woodland species like wild bleeding heart (*Dicentra eximia*), red baneberry (*Actaea rubra*), or green and gold (*Chrysogonum virginianum*). Shade, average to dry soils, zones 3–9.

Christmas fern emerging in spring

Little bluestem, *Schizachyrium scoparium*

One of the best warm-season grasses for New England gardens, little bluestem (*Schizachyrium scoparium*) has a number of great attributes that make it a fantastic alternative to the potentially invasive Chinese silvergrass (*Miscanthus sinensis*) commonly found in gardens. With the diversity of great plants at our fingertips, it would be impossible to choose a favorite graminoid (grass or grass-like plant) from the native flora, but most horticulturists agree that little bluestem is one of the best. It combines the ability to grow in some of the sunniest, driest sites New England has to offer with the ability to compete with strongly spreading species without being overly aggressive. Its versatility makes it a great choice either as a utilitarian solution, perhaps for stabilizing a slope, or for adding an accent of late fall color in an ornamental garden.

Like many of our native clumping grasses, little bluestem starts slowly, barely popping its head up in spring before growing quickly in the heat of summer. For this reason, we like to combine it with early(ish) season interest plants like sundial lupine (*Lupinus perennis*), bird's foot violet (*Viola pedata*), or three-toothed cinquefoil (*Sibbaldiopsis tridentata*). Summer through fall is the prime ornamental season for little bluestem. When the blue-green foliage begins to change to a darker silvery-purple, maturing to orange as the seeds ripen, it displays numerous tufts of silvery plumage that catch the sun and can be blinding in the right light. The display on a sunny, windy day is glorious and only gets better as the foliage matures to rich shades of bronze.

Little bluestem is one of those plants that looks best in masses, but it also works well as a specimen in more formal gardens. Sun, average to dry soils, zones 3–9.

Little bluestem

Prairie dropseed

Prairie dropseed, *Sporobolus heterolepis*

Prairie dropseed (*Sporobolus heterolepis*) is a wonderful mounding grass that stays shorter than most other warm-season clumping grasses. The foliage usually stays a little less than twelve inches tall, gently flopping over in a delicate mop-like pattern. The grass overall has great structure and can easily fit in between larger clumping perennials in a mixed border, or can be used to great effect as a lawn alternative when planted in a mass. There is a particularly impressive prairie dropseed lawn at Chanticleer, a pleasure garden in Wayne, Pennsylvania, that is stunning midsummer through winter.

Red to silver flowers appear in late summer into fall, stretching to as much as two feet tall from the center of the foliage mound. The lighter color of the flowers contrasts nicely with the rich green of the foliage before it turns from green to orange and eventually to a rich, deep bronze in fall.

Prairie dropseed is tolerant of full sun and dry soils, though it is equally happy in average garden soils. Pair it with short-lived perennials like black eyed Susan (*Rudbeckia hirta*) and spotted beebalm (*Monarda punctata*) that will seed themselves around and between the grassy mounds. No patch of prairie dropseed is complete without a little butterfly milkweed (*Asclepias tuberosa*), whose bright orange flowers and deep green foliage look amazing when paired together. Sun to part sun, average to dry soils, zones 3–9.

Vines and Lianas

In strict botanical terms, a vine is a climbing plant with no woody stem, whereas a liana is a climbing plant with a woody stem. Think of a vine as an herbaceous perennial whose stems climb and need support, and a liana as a climbing shrub. In New England, we have several examples of each, but using them well in a garden can sometimes be a challenge. In some cases, vines and lianas can be quite vigorous and difficult to use in a formal garden, but when properly sited, this distinct group of plants can fill an important niche in the garden, offering whimsy and a strong vertical element.

Virgin's bower, *Clematis virginiana*

Virgin's bower (*Clematis virginiana*), an example of a true vine, can easily be mistaken for the non-native sweet autumn clematis (*C. ternifolia*) at first glance, but where sweet autumn clematis is considered invasive in some areas of the United States, virgin's bower is an important host plant for various beneficial native insects in addition to being beautiful. The toothed leaves coat twining stems that are happy to twist around any available trellis, arbor, or shrub within reach. Small white flowers are produced in profusion in late summer to fall, followed by intricate fruits that are arguably more interesting than the flowers themselves.

The fruits are round in shape and resemble pinwheels made of small, extended branches that eventually dry and open to catch the wind or float downstream. They persist on the plant into the winter and make excellent decorations during the harvest season.

Virgin's bower fruits are perhaps showier than its flowers.

Virgin's bower is remarkably adaptable and can be found on stream-banks and lakesides as easily as in dryland shrub thickets or woodland edges. As long as adequate sun is available, this vine is sure to thrive in your garden. It looks especially nice when planted at the base of winter-berry holly (*Ilex verticillata*), where it can twine up the sparse stems of winterberry and the fruit of both plants can complement each other in fall. Plant it at the base of tough-stemmed, tall herbaceous plants like Joe-Pye weed (*Eutrochium* spp.), wingstem (*Verbesina alternifolia*), or New York ironweed (*Vernonia noveboracensis*), and they will climb up during the season and provide a late season accent after the taller plant is no longer in bloom. Sun to part shade, average to moist soils, zones 3–9.

Trumpet honeysuckle, *Lonicera sempervirens*

Trumpet honeysuckle (*Lonicera sempervirens*) is easily the best choice for a native ornamental liana (woody vine). It boasts a long season of interest, leafing out earlier than most other native plants and blooming late into fall. The stems grow quite quickly, looking for something to twine around, and will happily twist themselves into knots in search of support. The twisted mass of stems on an older trumpet honeysuckle makes an inviting site for birds, which frequently nest in the plants just outside the Horticulture Building at Garden in the Woods.

Trumpet honeysuckle

Trumpet honeysuckle flowers are exquisite, arranged in clusters of long, tubular yellow to red blossoms starting in early summer and blooming heavily throughout the warm months of summer. While it blooms most heavily in summer, trumpet honeysuckle continues to bloom well into fall, frequently flowering in eastern Massachusetts in September and October. There is not a single plant that attracts more hummingbirds than trumpet honeysuckle, whose flowers almost seem to have been designed specifically to appeal to them. Underplant trumpet honeysuckle with some beebalm (*Monarda* spp.), wild columbine (*Aquilegia canadensis*), and cardinal flower (*Lobelia cardinalis*) for the perfect hummingbird garden.

Fruiting follows quickly after flowering, with berries that range in color from yellow to orange to red. There is a short but wonderful period when each cluster of berries displays fruits in each color before they all turn bright red and attract dozens of birds. Sun to part sun, average soils, zones 4–9.

The fruits of trumpet honeysuckle are just as colorful as its flowers.

Virginia creeper, *Parthenocissus quinquefolia*

We often get funny looks from people for recommending Virginia creeper (*Parthenocissus quinquefolia*) as a garden plant. It has a bit of a reputation as a weedy, aggressive liana that lacks ornamental interest. But there is perhaps no better replacement for the non-native Boston ivy (*P. tricuspidata*) that adorns brick walls, fences, and houses throughout much of New England, and we think it's a shame more people don't call this one Boston ivy instead.

Virginia creeper is a vigorous plant with five-lobed leaves, blue berries, and outstanding fall color. Like other true climbing (versus twining) lianas, Virginia creeper has unique structures called holdfasts that allow it to attach itself to flat walls made of brick and stone. For this reason, it's a great choice for dressing up a drab concrete wall or providing bird habitat in a small urban garden. It is a vigorous grower and should be sited accordingly. While flowers are fleeting and hardly ornamental, the fall color on Virginia creeper ranges from deep purple to bright red and outlasts all but the longest-lived flowers. Plant it anywhere—full sun to full shade, dry to moist soils, but give it plenty of space to stretch.

Like most native plants, this one offers more support for local wildlife than its non-native cousin, Boston ivy. In addition to carbohydrate-rich berries (very important for birds in late fall), Virginia creeper also is a host plant for a variety of beneficial insects like the incredibly cool Pandora sphinx. Sun to shade, dry to moist soils, zones 3–9.

Virginia creeper

Fox grape, *Vitis labrusca*

Fox grape (*Vitis labrusca*) is unfortunately undervalued as a landscape plant and as an edible. Many folks who see fox grape growing in the wild or along a woodland edge don't realize this is an incredibly tasty fruit and the wild congener for the popular Concord grape. Fox grape's flavor is similar to that of Concord grape, but with a touch more tartness.

Unlike cultivated grapes, which are widely considered difficult to grow, fox grape will grow just about anywhere. Drought tolerant once established, and disease resistant, these grapes counter the argument that edible species are finicky. Plant fox grape anywhere you are looking for a liana that can quickly cover a vertical space like a wall, fence, or arbor, and admire the large, heart-shaped leaves. A large grape arbor with a few seats underneath will become a wonderful outdoor room complete with edible wallpaper and ceiling.

Not a fan of grapes? Leave them for the birds and instead enjoy the show and song provided by our feathered friends, or watch your vines closely to admire a number of different caterpillars and other beneficial insects that use the grapes for both food and habitat. Sun to part sun, average to dry soils, zones 4–8.

Wild grape

APPENDIX A: PLANT LISTS

Top Plants for Pollinators

- Pennsylvania sedge, *Carex pensylvanica*
- Aster, *Eurybia, Ionactis, Symphyotrichum*
- Joe-Pye weed, *Eutrochium* spp.
- Wild strawberry, *Fragaria* spp.
- Spicebush, *Lindera benzoin*
- Cardinal flower, *Lobelia cardinalis*
- Cherry, *Prunus* spp.
- Oak, *Quercus* spp.
- Goldenrod, *Solidago* spp.
- Highbush blueberry, *Vaccinium corymbosum*

Top Plants for Sunny Gardens

- Bearberry, *Arctostaphylos uva-ursi*
- Milkweed, *Asclepias* spp.
- Flowering spurge, *Euphorbia corollata*
- Bluets, *Houstonia caerulea*
- Wild bergamot, *Monarda fistulosa*
- Black-eyed Susan, *Rudbeckia* spp.
- Little bluestem, *Schizachyrium scoparium*
- Three-toothed cinquefoil, *Sibbaldiopsis tridentata*
- Prairie dropseed, *Sporobolus heterolepis*
- Bird's-foot violet, *Viola pedata*

Top Plants for Shady Gardens

- Black cohosh, *Actaea racemosa*
- Maidenhair fern, *Adiantum pedatum*
- Twinleaf, *Jeffersonia diphylla*
- Mountain laurel, *Kalmia latifolia*
- Solomon's plume, *Maianthemum racemosum*

- Virginia bluebells, *Mertensia virginica*
- Wild blue phlox, *Phlox divaricata*
- Great rosebay, *Rhododendron maximum*
- Rue anemone, *Thalictrum thalictroides*
- Foamflower, *Tiarella cordifolia* var. *cordifolia*

Top Plants for Dry Sites

- Butterfly milkweed, *Asclepias tuberosa*
- Stiff aster, *Ionactis linariifolia*
- Spotted beebalm, *Monarda punctata*
- Fragrant sumac, *Rhus aromatica*
- Black-eyed Susan, *Rudbeckia hirta*
- Little bluestem, *Schizachyrium scoparium*
- Wild senna, *Senna hebecarpa*
- Downy goldenrod, *Solidago puberula*
- Blue wood aster, *Symphyotrichum cordifolium*
- Lowbush blueberry, *Vaccinium angustifolium*

Top Plants for Moist to Wet Sites

- Chokeberry, *Aronia* spp.
- Rose milkweed, *Asclepias incarnata*
- Pawpaw, *Asimina triloba*
- Atlantic white cedar, *Chamaecyparis thyoides*
- Witch hazel, *Hamamelis virginiana*
- Inkberry, *Ilex glabra*
- Spicebush, *Lindera benzoin*
- Cardinal flower, *Lobelia cardinalis*
- Purple pitcher plant, *Sarracenia purpurea*
- Blue vervain, *Verbena hastata*

Top Plants for Songbirds

- American spikenard, *Aralia racemosa*
- Woodland sunflower, *Helianthus divaricatus*
- Eastern red cedar, *Juniperus virginiana*

- Scarlet beebalm, *Monarda didyma*
- Black cherry, *Prunus serotina*
- White oak, *Quercus alba*
- Flowering raspberry, *Rubus odoratus*
- Red-twig dogwood, *Swida sericea*
- Highbush blueberry, *Vaccinium corymbosum*
- Viburnum, *Viburnum* spp.

Top Groundcovers

- Bearberry, *Arctostaphylos uva-ursi*
- Pennsylvania sedge, *Carex pensylvanica*
- Wild strawberry, *Fragaria virginiana*
- Barren strawberry, *Geum fragarioides*
- Canada mayflower, *Maianthemum canadense*
- Long beech fern, *Phegopteris connectilis*
- Woodland phlox, *Phlox divaricata*
- Mayapple, *Podophyllum peltatum*
- Three-toothed cinquefoil, *Sibbaldiopsis tridentata*
- Foamflower, *Tiarella cordifolia* var. *cordifolia*

Edibles and Herbs

- Ramps, *Allium tricoccum*
- Shagbark hickory, *Carya ovata*
- American hazelnut, *Corylus americana*
- Woodland strawberry, *Fragaria vesca*
- Sunchoke, *Helianthus tuberosus*
- Fiddlehead fern, *Matteuccia struthiopteris*
- Wild bergamot, *Monarda fistulosa*
- Red raspberry, *Rubus idaeus*
- Highbush blueberry, *Vaccinium corymbosum*
- Fox grape, *Vitis labrusca*

Plants with Dramatic Fall Foliage

- Black chokeberry, *Aronia melanocarpa*
- American hazelnut, *Corylus americana*
- Flowering spurge, *Euphorbia corollata*
- Sweetgum, *Liquidambar styraciflua*
- Blackgum, *Nyssa sylvatica*
- Sourwood, *Oxydendrum arboreum*
- Fragrant sumac, *Rhus aromatica*
- Sassafras, *Sassafras albidum*
- Blueberry, *Vaccinium* spp.
- Witherod, *Viburnum nudum*

Plants with Strong Winter Interest

- Striped maple, *Acer pensylvanicum*
- Yellow birch, *Betula alleghaniensis*
- Shagbark hickory, *Carya ovata*
- Wintergreen, *Gaultheria procumbens*
- American holly, *Ilex opaca*
- Winterberry holly, *Ilex verticillata*
- Fiddlehead fern, *Matteuccia struthiopteris*
- Christmas fern, *Polystichum acrostichoides*
- Three-toothed cinquefoil, *Sibbaldiopsis tridentata*
- Red-twig dogwood, *Swida sericea*

APPENDIX B: ECOREGION MAP

LEVEL 3 ECOREGIONS
OF NEW ENGLAND

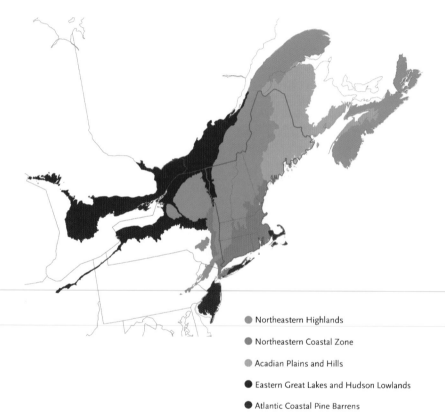

- Northeastern Highlands
- Northeastern Coastal Zone
- Acadian Plains and Hills
- Eastern Great Lakes and Hudson Lowlands
- Atlantic Coastal Pine Barrens

INDEX

ABOUT THE AUTHORS

New England Wild Flower Society Director of the Botanic Garden **Mark Richardson** studied ornamental horticulture at the University of Rhode Island and holds a master's degree from the University of Delaware's Longwood Graduate Program. *Native Plants for New England Gardens* is a product of his passion for native plants.

Photographer and author **Dan Jaffe** earned a degree in botany from the University of Maine, Orono, and has years of nursery and plant sales experience. He is the official propagator and stock bed grower for New England Wild Flower Society.

ABOUT NEW ENGLAND WILD FLOWER SOCIETY

New England Wild Flower Society's mission is to conserve and promote the region's native plants to ensure healthy, biologically diverse landscapes.

ABOUT GARDEN IN THE WOODS

The Society is based at Garden in the Woods, a naturalistic botanic garden of rare and common native plants, set on 45 acres.